The Boy Question

Following on from the huge success of *Boys Don't Try?* this essential new book answers nine key questions about how teachers and schools can best tackle boys' academic underperformance. For decades schools have grappled with the most significant barriers to male academic success: a lack of motivation to succeed, poor attitudes to learning, lower literacy levels and a reluctance to read for pleasure or write at length. In this compelling book, Mark Roberts provides clear answers about how teachers can tackle 'The Boy Question'.

Each chapter answers a frequently asked question about how best to teach boys, outlining the issue and demonstrating what can be done about it. Informed by a wealth of research and the author's personal experience of successfully teaching boys, this book offers an abundance of practical advice for the busy classroom teacher. It will shine a light on what makes boys tick and how we can design effective curriculums to ensure they can best acquire powerful knowledge.

With practical advice and examples to help address anti-school attitudes and stem the cycle of boys' underachievement, this is essential reading for all teachers and school leaders.

Mark Roberts is Director of Research at a school in Northern Ireland. Previously, he has worked at schools in Devon and Manchester. Mark writes books and articles about teaching and studying English and is also a frequent contributor to TES on subjects including pedagogy, behaviour, leadership and educational research.

'It's one thing to identify a problem, quite another to suggest some workable solutions. In *The Boy Question* Mark Roberts achieves the second with remarkable acuity. He provides compelling insights into why many boys are not achieving what they might, unpicks the research and provides really helpful suggestions for cracking some of the issues. This book is beautifully constructed; colleagues will find the research invaluable, particularly as it is translated into workable suggestions for the classroom. There are some hard hitting messages here, but Mark delivers them with such sensitivity and nuance that the proposals he suggests become utterly compelling.'

Mary Myatt
Education Thinker and Writer

'*Boys Don't Try?* proved a smash-hit with teachers because the authors tackled one of the biggest issues for teachers – the 'Boy Question' – with skill and a rich array of evidence. Mark Roberts returns to tackle the topic of boys in education with another terrific account of the struggles and successes of boys. With chapters from motivation to misbehaviour, to role models and writing, Roberts marshals' key evidence, slims down complex debates, and shares eminently practical approaches for the classroom. If you are seeking ways to ensure boys do better in your school, this is definitely the book for you.'

Alex Quigley
Author and National Content Manager at the
Education Endowment Foundation

'I loved this book. It is a grounded and balanced exploration of how we can work to support and challenge boys to aim high and fulfil their potential. It outlines some of the unhelpful assumptions and preconceptions which may hold us back from having ambitious aspirations for the boys in our classrooms, before going on to answer the question: "What can we do about it?"

The book is very well-researched and thoroughly referenced. It is up to date, offering insights into navigating the current pandemic. Its broad scope is reflected in the examples it includes from a range of different subject areas. Mark is eminently reasonable in his expectations with respect to teacher workload, showing how focussing on what is most effective can often correlate to adopting practices which are less labour- and time-intensive than our previous practice.

The Boy Question is strongly recommended for all those responsible for teaching, or raising, boys. It makes clear that considering the evidence, avoiding the pitfalls and following some of the suggested strategies will help the girls in our schools to succeed, too.'

Jill Berry
Former Head, now Leadership Development
Consultant and Education Commentator

The Boy Question

How to Teach Boys to Succeed in School

Mark Roberts

Routledge
Taylor & Francis Group

LONDON AND NEW YORK

First published 2022
by Routledge
2 Park Square, Milton Park, Abingdon, Oxon OX14 4RN

and by Routledge
52 Vanderbilt Avenue, New York, NY 10017

Routledge is an imprint of the Taylor & Francis Group, an informa business

© 2022 Mark Roberts

British Library Cataloguing-in-Publication Data
A catalogue record for this book is available from the British Library

Library of Congress Cataloging-in-Publication Data
Names: Roberts, Mark, 1977- author.
Title: The boy question : how to teach boys to succeed in school / Mark
  Roberts.
Description: Abingdon, Oxon; New York, NY : Routledge, 2022. | Includes
  bibliographical references and index. |
Identifiers: LCCN 2021058724 | ISBN 9780367509088 (hardback) | ISBN
  9780367509118 (paperback) | ISBN 9781003051787 (ebook)
Subjects: LCSH: Boys--Education. | Academic achievement. | Motivation in
  education. | Sex differences in education.
Classification: LCC LC1390 .R63 2022 | DDC 371.8211--dc23
LC record available at https://lccn.loc.gov/2021058724

ISBN: 978-0-367-50908-8 (hbk)
ISBN: 978-0-367-50911-8 (pbk)
ISBN: 978-1-003-05178-7 (ebk)

Typeset in Melior
by KnowledgeWorks Global Ltd.

Printed and bound by CPI Group (UK) Ltd, Croydon, CR0 4YY

For my parents

Contents

Acknowledgements

First, I'd like to thank everyone at Routledge for their enthusiasm and expertise during the writing of this book. Particular thanks must go to my editor, Annamarie Kino, for her calm and reassuring wisdom. Big thanks also go to Molly Selby.

I'd also like to offer my gratitude to the people who contributed such fascinating case studies to the book: Mark Enser, DeMarco Ryans, Freya Odell, Alice Visser-Furay and Lou Enstone.

Sincere thanks also go to readers of draft chapters – Alex Quigley, Mary Myatt, Jill Berry, Shaun Allison and Sarah Ledger – for their perceptive, encouraging and robust opinions. It would have been a lesser work without their advice. I'm also very grateful to Roz Burrows for her incredibly helpful comments and suggestions.

Thanks for everyone on Twitter who shares their thoughts and ideas politely and respectfully. Thanks also to all the teachers I've worked with, and all the brilliant boys and girls I've taught over the years. I've learnt a lot from you all.

Massive thanks to Matt Pinkett for the discussions about the contents and structure of the book, and for his valuable feedback on some of the early draft chapters. Chapter 6 in particular benefitted significantly from his input.

A big shout out to Jeff Flanagan for making my rubbish graphics look professional, and to Kevin Smith for artistic inspiration.

Finally, and most importantly, my heartfelt thanks to my wife, Harriett, and my sons Joe, Angus and Ned. Your love, support and extreme patience gives me both the space and determination to go upstairs and finish my 'boring books'.

Introduction

In a nondescript office in Westminster, a junior civil servant scans the columns of a multi-coloured spreadsheet. Noticing alarming swathes of red in one particular category, he picks up the phone and dials his boss.

In the conference room of a bog-standard Midlands comprehensive, a group of senior leaders fall into silence under the blinking strip lights, having just listened to the data manager's presentation on projected grades for the summer exam series.

A dozen miles down the road at a prestigious fee-paying school, a housemaster sits nursing a cup of tea in his study. Shaking his head, he reads the same list of names for his forthcoming Saturday morning homework detention.

And, in a primary school classroom in a deprived area of the North West, a young NQT is consoled by her professional mentor. Through tears of frustration and shame, she recounts the outrageous behaviour of some of the year 5 pupils in the afternoon session.

What are we going to do about...?

For decades now, scenes like the ones described above have been played out in classrooms, meeting rooms and offices across the country. The pattern is depressingly familiar. Once more, this most serious problem – the boy question – has been raised:

- *What are we going to do about the gender attainment gap?*

- *How can we improve boys' attitude towards school?*

- *What can be done about boys who don't work hard enough?*

- *Is there anything we can do about boys' lower literacy levels?*

- *How can I stop the behaviour of some boys ruining my lessons?*

The lockdown effect

With the release of *Boys Don't Try?* in April 2019, there came a renewed focus on issues of male academic underachievement. Offering a blueprint for rethinking how we educate boys, the ideas contained in that book were embraced by many teachers and school leaders. There was a sense of real purpose about the efforts to tackle the boy question, once and for all.

Then coronavirus happened

Since lockdown, media stories about boys dropping further behind have emerged almost weekly. A report from the National Foundation for Educational Research, for example, seems to confirm these fears.[1] According to their research, a survey of teachers 'found that 21 percent say that boys have fallen further behind normal expectations than girls'. By stark contrast, 'only 1 percent felt that girls had fallen behind'. Older boys in particular seem to have slipped back during the pandemic, as 'almost two fifths of secondary teachers reported that boys were more behind their usual learning levels than girls'. Because of boys' failure to keep up with distance learning, the authors of the report cautioned that 'targeted catch-up support may be required to ensure that gender gaps do not widen further'.

A pedagogy for change

Given the apparent slide in boys' progress, urgent action is required to make sure that boys aren't allowed to languish behind girls. *The Boy Question* offers the opportunity to recapture the impetus that *Boys Don't Try?* inspired among many working in education. The issues are clear. And, as this book is going to illustrate, the solutions are within our grasp.

There is a simple response to the thorny question of how we are going to solve the boy question.

That answer is… *you.*

The structure of the book

Each chapter of *The Boy Question* answers a frequently asked question about how best to teach boys. The format of these chapters follows an easy-to-navigate structure: *What's the issue?* and *What can we do about it?* Informed by a wealth of research, and my own experiences of successfully teaching boys, each chapter will offer an abundance of practical advice for the busy classroom teacher.

The opening section looks at how we can encourage boys to strive for academic excellence:

● Chapter 1 explains how popular approaches to motivating boys often backfire, offering instead a practical and sustainable approach to inspiring boys to achieve

- Chapter 2 considers how conflict can arise between teachers and boys, providing a blueprint for dealing with problematic classroom behaviours

- Chapter 3 evaluates the debate about using male teachers as role models for boys, suggesting the most useful ways to support and encourage our male students

The book's middle section focuses on how teachers can display and maintain high expectations of boys:

- Chapter 4 exposes the reality of boys' ineffective approaches to studying, demonstrating how we can help them adopt organised and impactful study habits

- Chapter 5 reveals how boys often receive unhelpful feedback from teachers, outlining more effective forms of feedback to boost boys' progress

- Chapter 6 explores common pedagogical pitfalls that lead to lower expectations of boys, highlighting steps we must take to ensure they are sufficiently challenged

In the final section of the book, the emphasis is on helping boys read more enthusiastically and become more skilful writers:

- Chapter 7 addresses boys' negative attitudes towards academic writing, recommending key strategies to improve their written communication

- Chapter 8 investigates reasons for the reading gap between girls and boys, putting forward a plan to get more boys reading for development and enjoyment

- Chapter 9 reflects on boys' aversion towards the creative writing taught in school, giving advice on how to get boys writing with imagination, precision and style

Getting boys back on track

By adopting the pedagogical techniques recommended in this book, you will get boys back on track. The classroom teacher is the most significant piece in this difficult puzzle. The purpose of *The Boy Question* is to help you teach in a way that will allow boys to flourish. Embracing research from education, psychology and cognitive science, it will shine a light on what makes boys tick and how they can most effectively acquire powerful knowledge. With a sound theoretical base, it will give you – the time-poor classroom teacher – a whole range of practical strategies to tackle your concerns about teaching boys effectively.

More motivated, resilient and productive; better organised and behaved; more sophisticated communicators; more knowledgeable and better equipped to learn independently. Wouldn't you love to start seeing all of these things in the boys that you teach?

Well, all you have to do now is turn the page and begin…

Note

1 Sharp, C., Nelson, J., Lucas, M., Julius, J., McCrone, T., & Sims, D. (2020) 'Schools' responses to Covid-19: the challenges facing schools and pupils in September', National Foundation for Educational Research: Nuffield Foundation. Available at: https://www.nfer.ac.uk/media/4119/schools_responses_to_covid_19_the_challenges_facing_schools_and_pupils_in_september_2020.pdf (Accessed 26th October 2020).

PART A
Motivating boys to work hard

How can I motivate boys to succeed in my classroom?

What's the issue?

In most countries of the world, across primary, middle and secondary education, girls get better grades. Current modelling indicates that a boy born in 2016 is 75% less likely to attend university than a girl born in that year.[1] In areas of the curriculum where boys have traditionally outperformed girls, girls have caught up or overtaken boys. In the UK, girls outperform boys in the majority of STEM[2] subjects, with 67% of girls achieving 9–4 (A*–C) grades, compared to 63% of boys. Even though boys are still ahead in the traditional male stronghold subjects of maths and physics, the boys now lead by just 1 percentage point.[3]

Boys lag behind girls academically for a variety of reasons. Peer pressure, teachers' negative expectations and counterproductive 'boys' engagement strategies' contribute to male academic underperformance.[4] In this chapter, we'll consider how academic motivation also plays a significant – often overlapping – part in holding boys back.

What is academic motivation?

You'd like to think that there is a simple answer to this simple question but, unfortunately, there isn't. Reviewing the research into academic motivation and gender isn't easy. Academics from different disciplines use a plethora of terms for the study of this concept and other related concepts. As well as academic motivation, we get *conscientiousness, deferred gratification, self-discipline, self-control, self-concept, self-regulation, inhibitory control, aspiration, goal-setting,* as well as opposites such as *impulsivity, immediate gratification, procrastination, self-handicapping ....*

For the purpose of academic research, these similar terms have precise definitions that can be useful in their own right. But for the benefit of the time-poor classroom teacher reading this section, while I'll use some of them at times where I think they can offer particular insight, in the main I'm going to collate this smorgasbord of terms together under the umbrella of **'motivation'**. For clarity, I'll be following the definition used by Professor Andrew Martin from University of New South Wales, who specialises in boys' academic motivation:

> Motivation can be conceptualised as students' energy and drive to learn, work effectively, and achieve to their potential at school and the behaviours that follow from this energy and drive.[5]

Anecdotally, teachers frequently tell me that in lessons, on the whole, girls are more willing than boys to embrace hard work and dedicate themselves to attaining the best possible grades. But does the evidence back up this belief?

Are girls more motivated to succeed in class?

In a 2013 study, German researchers Fischer et al. explored why female secondary students do better than male students. They found that:

> Females' advantage in final secondary school grades ... can be explained by [their] higher achievement motivation. Showing more compensatory effort as well as self-control and taking more pride in their own productivity helps females to outperform their male counterparts at secondary school.[6]

In other words, girls are generally less distracted than boys, are more driven to produce their best work and, in cases where they lack confidence in a subject, they put in *more* effort to make up for their perceived shortcomings, unlike boys who tend to overestimate their abilities and produce less work as a result. This finding supports previous studies that have shown that boys are more likely to overestimate and girls underestimate their academic competence.[7] Andrew Martin notes that research consistently reveals how:

> Girls are statistically significantly higher in learning focus, planning, study management, and persistence while boys are significantly higher in self-sabotage or self-handicapping.[8]

Research by Ablard and Lipschultz into the learning behaviours and attitudes of high prior-attaining seventh grade students in the US found that girls were far more likely to use metacognitive strategies and remain motivated when faced with setbacks than boys, especially when attempting 'tasks that were particularly difficult or tasks that involved reading and writing'.[9]

What motivates boys?

A 2014 study of over 400 Italian students ranging from age 9 to 22 found that *intrinsic motivation* 'tended to be stronger for females than for males across all educational levels'. Whereas girls are more likely to be driven by the belief that learning is an end in itself, boys are more driven by 'external regulation', whereby they are motivated by 'a valued end'.[10]

Intrinsic versus extrinsic motivation

When we have **intrinsic motivation**, our behaviour is driven by internal rewards. In other words, we are motivated to do something because we find it inherently satisfying. Boy A, for example, has learned to play the piano for the sheer joy of being able to appreciate the beautiful melodies of Debussy and Duran Duran.

By contrast, **extrinsic motivation** happens when we do something not because we find it satisfying or enjoyable but because we are keen to get something in return or avoid some form of negative consequence. So while Boy A is writhing with pleasure as he tinkles 'Save a Prayer' on his ivories, Boy B next door hates his piano lessons. The only reason he's learning the bloody piano is because his parents have promised him a puppy for Christmas if he sticks with it.

Why should this concern teachers?

What's the problem with boys lacking intrinsic motivation? Why does it matter if boys and girls are motivated to meet goals in different ways? Is there an issue if girls see the learning of coding as inherently worthwhile, while boys see it as a necessary step towards a highly remunerated career in the IT sector? Well, research consistently shows that extrinsic motivation is related to poor self-efficacy (confidence in one's ability), anxiety and lack of control.[11] What's more, we know from Ablard and Lipschultz's study, and several previous studies, that as well as lacking intrinsic motivation, boys were much more likely to set performance goals than mastery goals.[12] Research has shown that performance goals are less likely to lead to high-achievement outcomes than mastery goals.[13]

Performance goals versus mastery goals

According to psychologists, when humans set themselves achievement goals, they generally fall into two categories.

Students who follow **performance goals** are motivated by the prospect of receiving good grades. They are driven by the idea of outperforming others. They are more likely to be motivated by extrinsic factors. Generally, they prefer feedback that flatters them and choose tasks that make them look competent, while ducking ones that show up their weaknesses. When they fail at tasks, they are more likely to see the failure as a sign that they are lacking in ability and that they are going to fail in the future.

Students who adopt **mastery goals** are different. They are driven by the satisfaction of learning new knowledge and skills and getting better at a subject over time. They are intrinsically motivated and like feedback that helps them improve as a learner. Easy tasks leave them feeling bored, so they will opt for challenging activities if given a choice. They see failure as a learning opportunity and recognise that mastery of a subject requires not just effort but also plenty of practice.

In summary, the research about academic motivation tells us that a major reason why boys lag behind girls is because they are more likely to:

● overestimate their ability and do less work as a result

● lack resilience and avoid challenging tasks

● self-sabotage if they think they are likely to fail

● be extrinsically motivated

● follow performance goals

So what can the busy classroom teacher do to try and counter these attitudes and habits? How might they try and recalibrate the attitudes of boys in their lessons? What things could they start – and, perhaps, more pertinently, *stop* – doing to ensure that boys are motivated in a way that is going to give them the right mindset to thrive in their subject?

What can we do about it?

With the emergence of the gender attainment gap over the last few decades, schools have dedicated a great deal of energy and resources into trying to get their underperforming boys back on track. Some schools have managed to create an ethos where boys, on the whole, strive for academic success in a purposeful and effective way. In other schools, where boys are floundering, we can still find individual teachers who have managed to hold back the tides of apparent apathy and have helped to create islands of productivity and self-belief among the boys they teach. What are they doing that the others aren't?

Having scrutinised the research, having observed lots of teachers who get the most out of their male students and having had a fair amount of success teaching boys myself, here are the areas that I believe are key to effective academic motivation:

● **Focus on subject-specific success**

When faced with boys who avoid work in lessons and appear to lack aspirations in general, it's easy to make the assumption that the schoolY as a whole needs to act to inspire them to become motivated across the curriculum.

By the time they've reached year 11, how many 'Aspiration' assemblies have switched-off, underperforming boys had to sit through? You know the type. There's the obligatory low resolution YouTube video, featuring geese flying in V formation, or a hamstrung athlete hobbling over the finish line. The soundtrack is an 'uplifting' 1990s power ballad featuring the word 'Believe ...' in the title. Pseudo-profound slogans run in subtitles that are inspirational yet illogical: 'the more you want it, the more it wants you!'

While such rousing motivational assemblies tick all the SMSC[14] boxes and excite the average senior leader, they are far, *far* less effective in changing boys' habits than effective teaching which gives them challenging but achievable subject-specific goals.

Coe et al. point out in their 2014 guide to great teaching[15] that generic efforts to boost the motivation of struggling and disaffected learners:

> ...are unlikely to achieve that end. Even if they do, the impact on subsequent learning is close to zero.[16] In fact the poor motivation of low attainers is a logical response to repeated failure. Start getting them to succeed and their motivation and confidence should increase.

In *Boys Don't Try?*,[17] I provide a detailed explanation of why attempts to motivate boys through specific engagement strategies have been a disaster for boys' attainment. Instead of trying to 'hook' struggling or switched-off boys into learning through games, active learning or sport, to develop lasting academic motivation, you'll need to ensure students taste success in your subject so that they become keen to achieve further. As Muijs and Reynolds argue, '... the effect of achievement on self-concept is stronger than the effect of self-concept on achievement'.[18]

In order to get boys really wanting to do well, we need to forget about masking the subject content and apologising for what we are about to teach. Our job is, rather, to get them to appreciate the inherent beauty and joy of our subject by doing well in it, by getting a flavour of what it feels like to be a proper mathematician, historian, artist and ... err ... whatever it is that we call someone who does English at a high level. Harry Fletcher Wood sums this up beautifully:

> Self-efficacy – confidence in one's own abilities – is domain-specific: a student may feel brilliant at geography but hopeless in Spanish ... confidence and motivation will grow as [a teacher] shows them what success looks like and helps them to achieve it.[19]

Let's now consider what this might look like in your classroom.

● Use effective teaching strategies to make boys successful in your subject

In an important Australian study in 2002, Rowe and Rowe analysed attainment data from 270,000 secondary school students. They noted that while there were important gender differences in the data, there were also 'markedly large class/teacher effects'.[20] As Andrew Martin explains, 'what this implies is that addressing (gender-related) motivation and achievement issues is primarily tackled through quality pedagogy'.[21] This research – along with the examples cited above which show the need for a subject-specific focus – make it clear that the biggest motivational shifts for boys will mainly take place within the four sticky tack-stained walls in which you teach.

Whenever I talk to groups of teachers about the impact of success on boys' motivation, I always receive this very reasonable question in response:

How am I meant to get boys to be successful in my classroom, when they're switched off in the first place?

Here are some pedagogical principles that I recommend to get unmotivated boys tasting success:

Motivating boys tip 1: Feed for fulfilment

This strategy is not one for the educational purists. But I've found it highly effective in helping demotivated boys to feel like they can achieve in my subject (English). Here's how it works. You set the class off on a challenging activity. While they are working on it, you circulate and go to the boys who are switched-off or stuck. Provide a verbal or written scaffold to help them come up with a good response. Depending on how stuck they are, this might involve a helpful prompt or you effectively giving them a complete answer. When you revert back to whole class teaching, you make sure you call on these boys. Hey presto, they provide a decent answer!

To some, this seems like cheating. You're doing the work for them. They need to work it out for themselves. My response is this: first, this is effective teaching, in that you've provided them with the necessary knowledge for and the method of succeeding in this activity, which can be called upon in a similar task in future. Even if you've given them the answer, you will have made sure you explained how to arrive at that answer, so a model response has been given. Second, this is effective teaching, in that you've taken the decision to provide a short-term sense of achievement in order to motivate a reluctant boy to experience success in the subject. Over time, you'll need to do this less frequently. These boys will start to work it out for themselves. But only because you've shown them how, and made them feel like it's something they can do well in your class.

Motivating boys tip 2: Rephrase to amaze

When you call on unenthusiastic boys during questioning, you'll often get a fairly middling response:

TEACHER: *Adnan, can you tell me what happens when a volcano erupts?*

ADNAN: *Well, Miss, the ... err ... the ash and rocks all fly out. Sometimes it's little pieces and other times it's large rocks.*

Adnan's response is imprecise and lacking in technical terminology, but he's on the right line. At this point in the scheme of learning, the class have only done a few lessons on volcanoes. The teacher could probe deeper and would probably discover that Adnan couldn't remember what we call the things that come out during eruptions. Or, she might ask another super-keen pupil, who knows everything about everything, to provide this additional information. But, at this stage, this might make a further dent in Adnan's view of himself as an embryonic geographer. So, instead, the teacher decides to rephrase to amaze:

TEACHER: *Yes, you're right, Adnan. A volcanic eruption produces ash clouds, where small pieces of rock and glass are carried in the air. It also produces volcanic bombs – those larger bits of very hot rock that you mentioned.*

Notice how the teacher, without showering around empty praise, makes it seem like Adnan gave a fluent and confident answer. Also, they make it sound like he actually used the term 'volcanic bombs'. Over time, the teacher will make sure he does. But for now, he's buzzing from having 'given' such a good answer.

You can take this a stage further. In the next lesson, the teacher might refer to 'those volcanic bombs that Adnan told us about yesterday'. After a while, everyone starts to believe that Adnan is destined for a PhD in geology. It might seem a little bit like an Orwellian rewriting of history but, in my experience, 'rephrase to amaze' motivates boys beautifully.

Motivating boys tip 3: Let them write like you

To be good at something, we need to understand the full process, from initial stages to successful resolution. We'll be looking at how to improve boys' writing in much more detail in Chapter 6, but for now, let's consider how modelling can be used as a technique for developing boys' self-efficacy, by allowing them to experience the success of writing just like the teacher.

Providing model answers allows those reluctant boys to see what success looks like. It offers an incremental rising of challenge to emulate, allowing demotivated boys to gain confidence. Sometimes, though, when teaching a group of boys who are really turned off by writing, you need to orchestrate opportunities for them to experience successful writing.

An excellent way to do this is to get them to copy down your model answer in their exercise books. To work well, this must be done live, with you verbalising your thoughts as you make decisions about vocabulary, syntax and paragraph structure. You might argue that copying a whole paragraph down from the board is a waste of time. In most cases, I'd agree with you. We'll also be looking at time-wasting activities in Chapter 6. But in this case, the time spent copying down your work is a valuable investment. Not only have they had the benefit of listening to your expert thought processes, they've also – and this part is critical – been able to experience the satisfaction of writing something impressive in their book. This might well be a feeling that they've not encountered before. Yes, it's your work but they've channelled and begun to appropriate it.

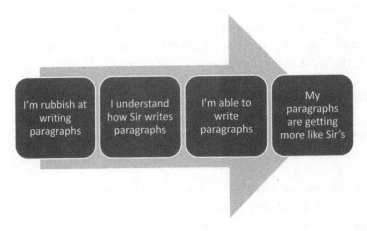

This works even better if it's a class model, co-constructed with input from pupils along the way. Over time, this worked example is something to go back to and use as a basis for future writing. *Remember the answer you wrote down from the other lesson? See if you can use that for the start of this answer …*

Gradually, they begin to understand what it takes to do well in this subject. They've had a flavour of success. Almost with noticing, they are becoming keen for a further taste.

● Make boys aware of their overconfidence

As we'll discover in Chapter 4, boys are more likely to overestimate their ability and therefore ease their foot off the effort pedal. Given this knowledge, teachers in each subject need to give them a tactful but accurate appraisal of their current working level. In addition to the effective study skills that will be discussed in Chapter 4, there are other quick pedagogical tricks we can use to make boys aware of their misleading view of their working level. For instance, Craig Barton suggests getting students to assign a confidence rating out of 10 next to their answers. This technique brings a couple of benefits. First, it gives the teacher insight into the students' confidence on a given topic. Second, and most importantly, it forces students to acknowledge the errors they make on high-confidence answers.

○ Aim for an 80% success rate

What kind of success rate should your students be achieving on the questions that you set them? According to Barak Rosenshine's four decades of research into effective teaching, the optimal success rate is a magic 80%.[22] Any lower and the work you're setting is likely to be too hard and a further dent to many boys' confidence and motivation. Any higher and your male students are likely to be coasting, congratulating themselves on another easy win. When the level of challenge is pitched correctly, boys begin to see that they are making progress over time. They make the significant shift from *not knowing much stuff to knowing quite a lot of stuff.* This changes reluctant boys' attitudes to lessons in specific subjects: the satisfaction of successful accumulation of knowledge and skills being cemented over time.

○ Be wary of praise

When faced with switched-off boys, it's tempting to shower them with praise for every small achievement. *Well done for getting your pen out! Yes, Ahmed, the main character in the play is called Macbeth – that's a wonderful answer! You've filled in the first question on the worksheet (the one that we already did together on the board); have a green reward point!*
Stipek's research from 2010 shows how:

> Praise for successful performance on an easy task can be interpreted by a student as evidence that the teacher has a low perception of his or her ability. As a consequence, it can actually lower rather than enhance self-confidence.[23]

Imprecise praise is also unhelpful. Research indicates that inconsistent and vague reward strategies leave students feeling confused and uncertain about what they did to receive a reward.[24]

By contrast, teachers who offer polite and precise critique of under-par work are viewed as more difficult-to-please. In the short-term, this might annoy boys with performance goals who prefer flattery over realism. They might not like it to begin with, but over time, boys recognise this as high expectations. Not long ago, a year 10 boy answered a question in one of my low stakes quizzes. 'Do I get a reward point for that?' he asked. My response was to tell him that his reward was me being impressed by his knowledge. He smiled. We moved on. Nobody has asked for a reward or explicit praise since. My classes can tell when I'm genuinely impressed.

○ Reconsider group work

Some teachers love group work. Some are even good at getting students to work collaboratively so that everyone contributes and works harmoniously together. In my experience, it takes a lot of time to train students to share the load and learn *more* as a cohesive unit. I worry that the opportunity cost of this training time means less time to do other, potentially more important things, like guided and independent practice. Research from 2008 by Shumow et al.[25] about homework preferences found that students find studying with friends more enjoyable than studying on their own. But, crucially, they also found that students concentrate more and put more effort in when studying alone. Might this also be true of classroom study? If you insist on the benefits of group work in your classroom, make sure that boys aren't using it as a chance for mental truancy or an opportunity for a social gathering.

● Promote an ethos of mastery over performance

Given the knowledge that boys are more likely to follow performance goals, which tend to limit – or even sabotage – their potential, as teachers we need to do everything we can to challenge and help amend that attitude. The language we use gives powerful messages to the boys we teach: when we give feedback on the quality of their work, when we discuss future assessments and ones they've just done and, perhaps most importantly, when we talk about their education and career prospects. To promote a mastery approach among boys, we need to:

○ Help them understand that frustration and failure are part of the learning process

An important message to give to our male students is that *learning can make us feel anxious, annoyed and angry.* That coping with difficulty is an important part of getting better at a particular subject. That often we learn more from failure than we do from success. In their recent overview of the research into academic achievement, Duckworth et al.[26] point to research that suggests that 'students try harder when they appraise the emotion of frustration as a sign that they are challenging themselves and improving'.[27] Imagine a scenario where a boy gets given back a test paper with a poor grade plonked in the top corner in a circle of crimson ink. He takes one look at it, screws it into a ball and lobs it across the room into your recycling box. As professionals, we take exception to that kind of behaviour. We feel the urge to discipline him for the apparent sign of disrespect. Disrespect for his learning and for your classroom. If it happens again, it will need to be tackled. But a more fruitful approach might be to fish it out of the box, smooth the paper out, and have a quiet word:

We all get frustrated when we find things hard. But I'm pleased you care about doing well in my class. Next time, work on the difference between aerobic and anaerobic respiration and you'll be taking it home to show your parents, not chucking it in my bin.

○ Encourage them to set specific and challenging goals

As we'll find out in Chapter 5, feedback that is diagnostic and requires action is more effective than vague comments that are left to hang on the page.[28] The same goes for the goals we set for students or, ideally, get them to set for themselves. Summarising the results of a 2002 study, Duckworth et al. explain that:

"do your best" exhortations were generally found to be less effective in motivating effort than encouraging the identification of specific and challenging goals.[29]

Look again at the words of the teacher who decided not to castigate the vexed young man for using his test paper for basketball practice. Rather than saying *you're just going to have to put more effort in if you're going to do better*, they offer specific areas for improvement. An even better response would have been to ask the boy to read the crumpled test paper and get them to identify key areas to work on, based on their feedback. To be most effective in improving academic attainment, goals need to be (a) short-term, (b) seen as important by the student and (c) set by the student.[30] Suggest the following basic outline of goal-setting:

So a poor goal might be:

I'm going to work hard and meet the required standard in KS2 Reading SATS.

And a good one might be:

Goal	I want to meet the required standard
Plan	During silent reading, I'll put down the David Walliams and stretch myself with challenging non-fiction
Rule	I read complex texts in school and easier texts before bed
Habit	Four challenging texts read in the last two weeks

By contrast, goals that are focused on the distant future, seen as insignificant by the student and are imposed on them by others are less likely to come to fruition. Think back to the yearly tales of desperate parents who have apparently bribed their disenchanted son with a promise of £100 for every GCSE passed. How many of those boys end up cashing in?

○ Focus on continuous gradual improvement

Instead of distant extrinsic rewards, like promises of a lucrative career in finance or dentistry, we need to maintain a shared discourse of continually getting better at something. Boys are more competitive than girls. But, as I illustrated in Chapter 1 of *Boys Don't Try?*, efforts to introduce competition into the classroom have proved to be counterproductive and have damaged the self-efficacy of boys who are already lagging behind. If you want to channel boys' competitive natures, use the idea of competing against our previous self (mastery) rather than our peers (performance). What might this look like?

Motivating boys tip 4: Show how far they've come

In the hamster wheel experience of being a school student, it's easy to lose track of our progress. RAG[31]-graded numbers on our report card can tell us surprisingly little about whether we're getting better at something over time. For this reason, to motivate boys, give them a clear example of their improvement over time. Here's an example:

CALLUM: *I'm rubbish at essay introductions.*

TEACHER: *Well, you might think that but it's not accurate. It's January now, right? Let's go back and look at your introductions from September. They were pretty ropey, but you're miles better now than you were then! If you work on the feedback I've given you – specifically about embedding micro quotations and responding to the key words in the question – then by May your introductions are going to be very impressive.*

● **Be patient and work together on their self-control**

How long does it take you to form a desired new habit? You've decided you want to torture yourself lugging kettle bells about the gym five times a week. Or improve your pallid complexion by eating more of those things called vegetables. Or finally stop boring everyone with your convoluted plot and actually get started on that long-shelved novel. How long will you need to get from slob to slim, from burgers to broccoli, from talker to writer? According to research conducted in 2010 at UCL by Lally et al., the answer is *at least two months*. On average participants in the study took 66 days to start automatically performing the new habit.[32] So don't be too disappointed if the boys you teach slip up or take a while to start showing signs of consistent academic motivation. According to Lally et al. the odd setback won't stop a determined individual from achieving better habits. Only if they really lack control and are very inconsistent in their behaviours will the habit fail to stick.

In the battle against male academic demotivation, 'control' is a key word. When dealing with low-confidence boys who are scared of failure, we need to instil a feeling that they can influence their own outcomes and shape their own academic destiny. Remind them of how far they've come. Look back, for instance, at previous low stakes quizzes where they were getting 3/10 and now they're averaging 6–7 out of 10. Compare the work they produced in September with the work they're now crafting in February. When boys begin to taste success and appreciate the progress they've made, they start to buy in to the idea that they have control over how far they'll go in your subject.

A further influence on the motivation of individual boys is the feeling of belonging to a group who share a unifying sense of purpose. When we feel part of a group we are motivated by a desire to see our peers do as well as us, rather than trying to outdo them in a test.[33] In shifting boys' attitudes away from self-destructive performance goals and towards healthy and purposeful mastery goals, we can foster a classroom culture where all students are keen to do their best, and can recognise and celebrate the best in others.

How can I motivate the boys I teach to succeed?

STEPS TO SUCCESS

1 **ENABLE** Enable them to taste success in your subject

2 **HELP** Help them see their overconfidence

3 **DON'T** Don't use praise to motivate

4 **FOCUS** Focus on personal best

5 **HABIT** Goal > Plan > Rule > Habit

Notes

1 Hillman, N., & Robinson, N. (2016) 'Boys to men: the underachievement of young men in higher education – and how to start tackling it', Higher Education Policy Institute, Report 84. Available at: https://www.hepi.ac.uk/wp-content/uploads/2016/05/Boys-to-Men.pdf (Accessed 9th April 2020).

2 The acronym stands for 'science, technology, engineering and mathematics' and refers to any subjects that fit into this category.

3 wisecampaign.org.uk (2020) 'Analysis of GCSE STEM entries and results', Available at: https://www.wisecampaign.org.uk/statistics/analysis-of-gcse-stem-entries-and-results-2/ (Accessed 9th April 2020).

4 For a more detailed explanation of these issues, see Pinkett, M., & Roberts, M. (2019) *Boys Don't Try? Rethinking Masculinity in Schools*, Abingdon, Oxon: Routledge.

5 Martin, A.J. (2002) 'Motivation and academic resilience: developing a model of student enhancement', *Australian Journal of Education*, 46, pp. 34–49.

6 Fischer, F., Schult, J., & Hell, B. (2013) 'Sex differences in secondary school success: why female students perform better', *European Journal of Psychology of Education*, 28:2, pp. 529–543.

7 For example, Cole, D.A., Martin, J.M., Peeke, L.A., Seroczynski, A.D., & Fier, J. (1999) 'Children's over- and underestimation of academic competence: a longitudinal study of gender differences, depression, and anxiety', *Child Development*, 70:2, pp. 459–473.

8 Martin, A.J. (2004) 'School motivation of boys and girls: differences of degree, differences of kind, or both?', *Australian Journal of Psychology*, 56:3, pp. 133–146.

9 Ablard, K.E., & Lipschultz, R.E. (1998) 'Self-regulated learning in high-achieving students: relations to advanced reasoning, achievement goals, and gender', *Journal of Educational Psychology*, 90:1, pp. 94–101.

10 Vecchione, M., Alessandri, G., & Marsicano, G. (2014) 'Academic motivation predicts educational attainment: does gender make a difference?' *Learning and Individual Differences*, 32, pp. 124–131.

11 Vallerand, R.J., Pelletier, L.G., & Koestner, R. (2008) 'Reflections on self-determination theory', *Canadian Psychology,* 49:3, pp. 257–262.

12 Ibid.

13 For example, Schunk, D.H. (1996) 'Goal and self-evaluative influences during children's cognitive skill learning', *American Educational Research Journal*, 33:2, pp. 359–382.

14 Spiritual, moral, social and cultural development. Ofsted check how well schools teach this stuff to their pupils.

15 Coe, R., Aloisi C., Higgins, S., & Elliot Major, L. (2014) *What Makes Great Teaching? Review of the Underpinning Research.* Sutton Trust/Durham University, p. 23.

16 Gorard, S., See, B.H., & Davies, P. (2012) *The Impact of Attitudes and Aspirations on Educational Attainment and Participation.* York: Joseph Rowntree.

17 Pinkett, M., & Roberts, M. (2019) *Boys Don't Try? Rethinking Masculinity in Schools.* Abingdon, Oxon: Routledge.

18 Muijs, D., & Reynolds, D. (2011) *Effective Teaching: Evidence and Practice*, 3rd edition. London: Sage, p. 148.

19 Fletcher Wood, H. (2018) *Responsive Teaching: Cognitive Science and Formative Assessment in Practice*, Abingdon, Oxon: Routledge.

20 Rowe, K.J., & Rowe, K.S. (2002) 'What matters most: evidence based findings of key factors affecting the educational experiences and outcomes for girls and boys throughout their primary and secondary schooling'. Supplementary submission to House of Representatives Standing Committee on Education and Training: inquiry into the education of boys. Canberra, Australia: Department of Education, Training and Youth Affairs.

21 Ibid.

22 Rosenshine, B. (2012) 'Principles of Instruction: research based principles that all teachers should know', *American Educator*, Spring 2012.

23 Stipek, D. (2010) 'How do teachers' expectations affect student learning?', Available at: http://www.education.com/reference/article/teachers-expectations-affect-learning/ (Accessed 11th April 2020).

24 Thompson, T. (1994) 'Self-worth protection: review and implications for the classroom', *Educational Review*, 46, pp. 259–274.

25 Shumow, L., Schmidt, J.A., & Kackar, H. (2008) 'Adolescents' experience doing homework: associations among context, quality of experience, and outcomes', *The School Community Journal*, 2008, 18:2, pp. 9–27.

26 Duckworth, A.L., Taxer, J.L., Eskreis-Winkler, L., Galla, B.M., & Gross, J.J. (2019) 'Self-control and academic achievement', *Annual Review of Psychology*, 70, pp. 373–399.

27 Eskreis-Winkler, L., Shulman, E., Young, V., Tsukayama, E., Brunwasser, S.M., Duckworth, A.L. (2016b) 'Using wise interventions to motivate deliberate practice', *Journal of Personality and Social Psychology*, 111, pp. 728–744.

28 We'll be looking in detail at how feedback can be used to improve boys' attainment in Chapter 5.

29 Locke, E.A., & Latham, G.P. (2002) 'Building a practically useful theory of goal setting and task motivation: a 35-year odyssey', *American Psychologist,* 57:9, pp. 705–717.

30 Ibid.

31 Red-Amber-Green

32 Lally, P., van Jaarsveld, C.H.M., Potts, H.W.W., & Wardle, J. (2010) 'How are habits formed: modelling habit formation in the real world', *European Journal of Social Psychology*, 40:6, pp. 998–1009.

33 See, for example, Liem, G.A.D., & Martin, A.J. (2011) 'Peer relationships and adolescents' academic and non-academic outcomes: same-sex and opposite-sex peer effects and the mediating role of school engagement', *British Journal of Educational Psychology*, 81, pp. 183–206.

2 How should I react to boys who misbehave in my classroom?

What's the issue?

The tale I'm about to tell is an unsettling one. It's a sensational, once-in-a-generation story that occupied thousands of newspaper column inches and hours of national TV news footage. Fortunately, for students and teachers, this kind of thing happens very rarely...

In July 2009, Peter Harvey, a science teacher working at a secondary school in Nottinghamshire, attacked one of his students, a 14-year-old boy, about the head with a metal dumbbell weighing 3 kilograms. The boy sustained serious injuries: a fractured right temple bone and bleeding on the brain. During the trial, the court saw footage of the incident, filmed by a fellow pupil on her mobile phone. The boy called his teacher a 'bald-headed bastard' and told him to 'f**k off'. Witnesses reported that Mr Harvey dragged his pupil out of the classroom by his collar, then struck him twice with the heavy instrument, shouting 'die, die, die' as he lay on the floor.

Taking into account how Mr Harvey had been goaded by members of the class over a sustained period of time, and his fragile mental health leading up to the assault, the jury cleared the teacher of attempted murder. At sentencing, the judge imposed a two-year community service order for the lesser charge of grievous bodily harm.

What causes teacher anger?

It's widely accepted that teaching is a stressful job.[1] As Taxer et al. note,[2] teachers are more susceptible to emotional exhaustion – a key symptom of burnout – than those working in many other professions.[3] So what are the causes of teachers' emotional exhaustion? The evidence is clear: excessive workload and poor behaviour.[4]

Perhaps the saddest thing about these gloomy statistics is that one of the main *causes* of teachers' emotional exhaustion – some of the young people they work with – is also one of the main reasons why they opted to train to become teachers in the first place. It shouldn't really need saying, but those same teachers who lose their teaching mojo, and end up screaming repeatedly at the students they teach, largely chose to become teachers because they wanted to work closely with students.[5] At some time or other, they will also have put considerable effort into attempting to develop caring relationships with students.[6] Let me be clear: the vast majority of teachers I've met or worked with actually like children!

So what goes wrong? How does a bright-eyed and optimistic teacher, in love with their subject and keen to help children do well academically end up being a red-eyed misanthrope, threatening kids with all manner of medieval punishments if they don't sit down and shut up? Well, one thing in particular corrodes away at the teachers' soul: anger. It dampens their zest for teaching, affects their relationships with students (especially boys) and, ultimately, it impacts negatively on their results.

How common is teacher anger?

The Harvey case is an extreme example of teacher anger. But how frequently do teachers display lesser forms of anger in their classrooms? How often do teachers feel the proverbial red mist descending?

It's important to state from the outset that in life in general, anger is the most frequently displayed negative emotion. Given that teachers are humans as well (despite what some of our students may believe), this is also true of them.[7] A 2015 study into the feelings of 135 Bavarian classroom teachers found that, on average, they felt 'enjoyment in 97%, anger in 44% and anxiety in 25% of all their class periods'.[8] The study's sample included plenty of experienced teachers, who had an average of 15 years' experience of life at the whiteboard. These findings imply that while these teachers found something to enjoy in the vast majority of their lessons, 'anger and anxiety [were] also integral parts of teachers' classroom experiences'. We can all reflect on the horror class of our NQT year, bestowed on us by a sadistic timetabler, presumably for some unmentionable sin committed in a previous teaching life. And yet these results suggest that although these nightmare groups linger in our memory like a traumatic childhood trip to the dentist, in reality, most classes don't fit that kind of description. Across the typical week, teachers might feel pleased, frustrated and concerned during the same 60-minute lesson. Enjoyment and anger are bedfellows. If the ratios from this study can be taken as a very rough guide, for every couple of students that leave you feeling pleased and contented with the world, you'll encounter another one who will prove to be quite annoying. And the sad truth is that, for most teachers, the student that pushes their buttons is more likely to be male.

Teacher anger and gender

According to a 2019 study by Burić and Frenzel, teachers' emotions are based on judgements about whether student behaviour corresponds with the classroom goals we set:

> For example, it has been shown that teachers experience anger when students fail and teachers appraise this failure as caused by intentionally low effort invested by the students, or when teachers' instructional goals are obstructed by students' seemingly deliberate misbehaviour...or lack of motivation and commitment.[9]

As illustrated in *Boys Don't Try?*,[10] despite generally professing that there is no reason why boys can't do as well as girls in school, teachers tend to have lower expectations of boys and see boys' behaviour as more problematic than that of girls, even when similar behaviour occurs. Indeed, research into teacher-student relationships[11] supports this point. From the perspective of teachers, 'across grade levels, boys tend to form more conflictual relationships with their teachers than do girls'.[12] Generally, teachers expect less of boys, in terms of academic potential. They also expect boys to have worse behaviour than girls, so tend to pick up on it more readily. And to make things worse, this is particularly true of boys who are academically underperforming, especially when they come from a disadvantaged background.

We know, for instance, from research into setting that boys are far more likely to be consigned to bottom sets.[13] We also know that 'students from lower socio-economic backgrounds are over-represented in bottom groups'.[14] Furthermore, we have evidence that children with lower prior attainment, and those with lower levels of socioeconomic status, are more likely to experience teacher-student conflict.[15] So, according to the research, if you find yourself, for example, teaching a difficult class comprising mainly disadvantaged, struggling boys, unless you're careful and take steps to avoid becoming angry, you'll be more likely to come into conflict with them more than your colleague down the corridor who has a class populated with mainly advantaged, higher prior attaining girls.

The effects of anger on teachers

When teachers feel angry with the students they teach, the impact is profound. Teachers who frequently get angry have higher levels of emotional exhaustion. And research into the effects of emotional exhaustion on teacher performance and wellbeing shows that this leads to (a) low job motivation, (b) a lack of confidence in one's teaching ability,[16] (c) a greater likelihood of leaving the profession[17] and, unsurprisingly (d) a poor quality of teaching,[18] as anger interferes with teachers' ability to plan effectively and distracts their attention away from classroom tasks.[19]

The effects of teacher anger on students

It's easy to forget sometimes just how influential teachers are. As well as trying to make children cleverer, we also spend a lot of time shaping their character. Often, we do this unconsciously. And we don't just teach and develop relationships with individual students. For most of our time, we interact with 20-odd students and, invariably, we are the central focus in the room. As Farmer et al. put it, 'teachers' own social and emotional functioning impacts classroom quality and students' school adjustment'.[20] In other words, how we behave has a big effect on how our students will feel and how well they will learn. Or to put it another way, as teachers, our behaviour is highly contagious.

> According to psychologists, as humans we often involuntarily 'catch' behaviours and attitudes from other individuals that we are connected with. They call this **social contagion** theory. Everyday examples of contagious behaviour include yawning, laughing and those hilarious cat memes that Clive the data manager keeps sending by group email. Social contagion can work negatively, in the form of peer pressure, for example, where a girl might unconsciously start smoking to fit in with a group of rebellious friends. Or it can work positively. A boy who previously disliked chemistry might pick up his friend's passion for the subject and find himself working harder and enjoying it more over time.

Anyone who has watched the influence that one child can have over another group of children, just through their mere presence, will recognise the contagious nature of child-to-child relationships. Social contagion, however, doesn't just apply to students. As researchers into social contagion within education make clear, 'contagion is also present between teachers and students'.[21]

Negativity spreads

As with problematic social contagion between children, teachers can also be unwitting spreaders of negativity. A 2016 study by Oberle and Schonert-Reichl found that elementary school students had higher morning cortisol levels, and were therefore feeling more stressed, when their teacher had a higher level of burnout.[22] Stressed teachers, it would appear, unwittingly create an environment that makes for stressed kids.

Research also shows that teachers who are excessively autocratic in their teaching and 'attempt to motivate students by exerting pressure on them', through threatening language and harsh, public criticism, reduce their intrinsic motivation for learning. As we saw in Chapter 1, improving boys' intrinsic motivation is a key area if we are to reduce gender attainment gaps. Being warm and personable when being strict helps motivate boys to want to learn for learning's sake, rather than working only to avoid punishment.

Furthermore, there's a compelling body of research to suggest that when teachers conduct themselves in an aggressive manner, there is a negative impact on both student motivation and cognitive learning.[23] For example, a higher education study found lower levels of comprehension in classes where teacher behaviour was perceived to be inappropriate.[24] Why the students became unwilling or unable to perform for an uncivil teacher is unclear. Yet, it would appear that a vexed and confrontational teaching persona can contribute to negative learning outcomes.

Teacher anger: Who gets the blame?

The reason why students down tools – metaphorically or otherwise – for teachers who lose their temper can perhaps be explained by a fascinating 2004 study into the effects of teacher anger on students by McPherson and Young. Their research revealed that students are able to 'acknowledge that something they did evoked their teacher's feelings of anger'.[25] Yet, intriguingly, they also found that when teachers shout and threaten, despite being aware that they contributed to the anger, students are nonetheless far more likely to blame the teacher for the resulting outburst. In this situation, they make harsh judgements about the teachers' life circumstances, personality traits, or teaching competence:

> Essentially, even when students cause the teacher to feel angry, students believe the teacher is responsible when that anger is expressed. In short, students recognise that teachers get angry and that they are sometimes the reason for their teachers' anger, but they are less sympathetic when assigning attributions to the expression ...of this emotion.

Indeed, when it comes to teacher anger about students' poor performance, students tend to increase the proportion of blame they assign to the teacher. Put simply, if you get really cross with boys for not doing well on a test, unfairly or not, they're likely to think that it's mainly your fault. Give a boy a proper roasting for not trying on his mock SATs paper and he'll probably think that your lessons didn't help him learn the content. Or, even worse, if you're a female teacher, he might well cast sexist aspersions about you being moody because your period has landed.

What can we do about it?

Like it or not, the way we respond to the poor behaviour or effort of some boys is absolutely crucial. No matter how frustrating the behaviour of a particular boy or group of boys, our reaction will dictate whether the behaviour is likely to happen again.

Using the research into teacher anger and classroom conflict, as well as my own experience of teaching many tricky boys, I recommend the following steps to improving classroom behaviour:

● **Adopt a calm and open teaching persona**

In a significant 1994 study into anger and communication,[26] Laura K. Guerrero placed expressions of anger into four categories. Applying these categories to a classroom setting for their 2003 study, McPherson et al.[27] exemplified these as:

Distributive-aggression (direct and threatening)	Integrative-assertion (direct but non-threatening)
• Shouting	• Honestly articulated thoughts and feelings
• Criticising	• Not blaming the other person
• Threatening	• Considering other person's needs
• Abusive language	• Firm but fair
• Trying to 'get even'	• Trying to 'patch things up'
Passive-aggression (indirect but threatening)	**Non-assertive denial (indirect and non-threatening)**
• Something is wrong but no discussion	• Inability or unwillingness to confront thoughts and feelings
• Unclear what the problem is	• Hiding intense emotions
• Silent treatment	• Deny they are angry or that problems exist
• Coldness/dirty looks	
• Walking away	

McPherson et al.'s research supported the findings from Guerrero's earlier study. They found that how students respond to a teacher losing their temper depends on two key factors: 1) how the anger is displayed and 2) the intensity of the emotion. Anger that emerges as *distributive-aggression*, such as yelling and intimidation, or *passive-aggression*, such as sarcasm and indirect threats are generally viewed by students as unacceptable forms of teacher conduct, especially when expressed at high intensity. For this reason, using these forms of communication to deal with a student who has left you feeling vexed won't have the impact you were hoping for. Put simply, misbehaving boys won't change their behaviour if you are hostile, whether your attitude is expressed directly or indirectly. Nor, according to this research, will they modify their behaviour if you try to ignore behaviour and plough on through your teaching, using *non-assertive denial*, smiling grimly as the noise levels escalate. Tactically ignoring certain behaviours might work in some cases, but trying to pretend there isn't a behaviour problem will soon leave you foundering.

What really works…

So how do we improve boys' conduct? As human beings, teachers will inevitably become irked by some inappropriate behaviour. What's the best way to react when we feel our blood begin to bubble beyond the simmer stage? McPherson et al. make it clear that only one form of response is seen by students as reasonable and, crucially, is likely to have the desired effect of getting them to improve their conduct: *integrative-assertion*. This is communication that is clear and direct but non-threatening to the recipient. McPherson et al. advise that:

> Teachers should avoid intense, aggressive anger displays, and instead assertively discuss the problem with the class, try to be fair and open, and take into account students' reactions.

What might this look like in a lesson where you find yourself coming into conflict with some difficult boys?

The case of the flying biro

You're helping a student who is stuck when a pen comes flying across the room and hits you on the arm. With your back to most of the class, it's difficult to pin point which student propelled the object in your direction. You're not at all happy. Why would you be? When it comes to health and safety, teachers love to hyperbolise. *That could've taken someone's eye out!* But in this case it really could have. In the fraction of a second that these thoughts ricochet around your overheating brain you notice Ben – a boy with a history of defiant behaviour – appearing to suppress a giggle.

Now, notice the difference between the following two responses to the aftermath of the projectile incident:

TEACHER A: *BEN! How dare you laugh at me? That could've taken my eye out. GET OUT OF MY ROOM!*

This response is understandable but ultimately self-defeating. It pours fuel on the fire. This will probably lead to an escalation of poor behaviour that could derail the entire lesson.

TEACHER B: *I don't know who threw that but I know which direction it came from. Throwing a pen across my room is totally unacceptable behaviour. It's dangerous and reckless – even if it wasn't aimed at me and was only being passed to someone else. There's no excuse for it. There will be a consequence. I'm very disappointed. I will be speaking to these two tables about it at the end of the lesson, when I would very much appreciate it if whoever threw it owns up. We now need to get back on with our work.*

By contrast, this teacher's response follows an important piece of advice for dealing with poor behaviour from boys.

Behaviour tip 1: Turn down the heat

As soon as you feel your heat start to rise, you need to pause. Try and do nothing for a few seconds. Take time to think about what you're going to say and do next.

Teaching involves making hundreds of quick decisions each day: *Do I allow her to go to the toilet? Is he stuck or avoiding work? Is that a good enough answer? Shall I digress here, or carry on with my planned explanation?* With experience, these decisions come easily. They aren't made in anger.

But decisions about how to deal with anger-inducing behaviour can be high-stakes. These decisions can bring lasting consequences. The audience are poised, waiting to see what happens next. Your reaction – and how you frame this reaction – is key.

So, take your time. Like any good referee, have a deep breath before you start reaching for a card. Calmly and clearly manage the situation. Don't react without pausing to answer the following questions:

○ Am I following the behaviour policy?

○ Is my instinctive response fair and consistent?

○ Will my actions defuse or inflame the situation?

○ What's the best way to phrase this?

You've turned down the heat. Now you can make the right decision.

Shout, shout, let it all out?

Another common lesson context. The class are getting noisier. You're trying to help a stuck student but you can't really hear what they're saying. The hum becomes a buzz. The buzz becomes a wall of chatter. The wall of chatter becomes intolerable, a cacophonous pounding that hurts your ears and brings perspiration to your skin. Picking the loudest offender you can spot, you yell 'BE QUIET JAMES!'. The boy in question reddens and, for a moment, silence comes. But before long, like the persistent drone of a bloodthirsty mosquito, the hum of the class returns…

Behaviour tip 2: Raise the bar, not your voice

As we'll discover in Chapter 4, high levels of noise hinder cognitive processes. Maintaining noise levels that are conducive to learning, therefore, is an essential part of your job. But shouting is not the answer, for the following reasons:

● It leads to a 'noise arms-race'. Each time you shout out instructions, they respond in kind. You end up talking to them in a perpetually raised voice, which is bad for their comprehension, and your sanity

● It causes resentment and destroys long-term relationships with boys[28]

● It can scare or upset students who were trying to get on with their work

- It can have a negative impact on students with sensory triggers, such as students with autism

- It makes you look unprofessional in the eyes of your pupils

- It can damage your vocal chords

And, most importantly of all…

- It doesn't actually work

A few years back, I taught a very difficult bottom set GCSE English class, full of boys. At the start of the year, swearing, shouting out and fights were not uncommon. It was an exasperating time. During most lessons, I could feel my armpits moisten and my adrenaline levels rise. But I never shouted. Not once. I followed the policy rigidly and removed boys who caused repeated distraction. When the noise levels reached a critical mass, and the warnings were being ignored, I simply went and sat down in my chair. Folding my arms, I sat in silence and displayed an 'I've had enough of this' look. This became a visual cue: I have stopped teaching and will not continue until I have your full attention. After a minute or so, they eventually stopped talking. At this point I would say:

> *I really enjoy teaching this class[29] but when some of you choose to behave in this manner, there's nothing I can do to help you learn. I expect you to show respect, by not talking when I'm talking and by listening politely to each other. I will not speak over you. I expect you to work hard each lesson because I have high expectations of what you can achieve in this subject. At the moment, some of you are letting yourselves down. If this continues, you'll be going elsewhere. I don't want that to happen. I'd much rather have you in my class, learning. I'd like to apologise to those of you who have done everything I've asked of them this lesson. I'm sorry you're having to listen to this. Thank you for your patience. Right… Let's get back to the important thing I was teaching you.*

Resetting the temperature

By resetting the classroom temperature, I raised the bar of expectations and made it clear that I wouldn't tolerate this level of distraction. Over time, the class began to comply and the walks to my chair and subsequent pep talks became much rarer. One day, one of the boys – a clever but volatile young man who should have been in a higher group – asked me why I never shouted at the class. Most other teachers, he told me, ended up losing it with this class. I said that it wouldn't make any difference and he agreed. The class found my calmness odd, he said, but they appreciated not being shouted at. In the end, most of them did well at GCSE English.

Let's consider another frequently played-out scenario. At the start of the lesson, you give a boy a lateness warning, prompting him to answer back. He mutters something under his breath, which is probably 'That's so stupid', but is possibly 'You're so stupid'. You're fuming.

Did he just call me stupid?

Often, these situations escalate swiftly. A teacher communicating through distributive-aggression will move straight to confrontation mode. *Did you just call me stupid? I've got two degrees and a masters. You, however, are going to fail your GCSEs.*

Or they might try and get back at the cheeky boy by giving another warning, leading to a removal to an isolation room. This might well be a Pyrrhic victory: the boy will be back in the teacher's next lesson, still brooding at what he sees as an unfair warning followed by a reactive scattergun expulsion. A boy mumbling something about you under your breath can be infuriating. But responding to it in this way is self-defeating.

So, what would be a better way to manage this situation?

Behaviour tip 3: Don't make it about you (but don't make it about them either)

When we take a child's petty or vindictive comment to heart and respond with verbally aggressive behaviour, we lose not just the moral high ground. We also sabotage our chances of achieving what we want most of all: no repeat of the disrespectful behaviour.

Try to avoid taking things personally. Most behaviour is not really about you. This boy doesn't actually think you or, more likely, your decisions are stupid. He's just unable to contain his frustration at getting himself into trouble. Deal with this by using integrative-assertion communication and he'll usually concede that his attitude was out of order. To do this successfully, you need to take the individual boy out of the situation. Avoid making the behaviour specifically about him, by raising the bar with the class as a whole, reminding them of your expectations and the need for them:

> *I know some of you feel frustrated when you get given warnings for lateness. But, as I reminded you last lesson, when you miss the start of the retrieval activity you put yourself at a big disadvantage. You miss out on the opportunity to go over things we've done previously. I would be harming your chances of succeeding in this subject if I let you wander in 5 minutes late every lesson. I'm not prepared to do that. That's why I'll always give a warning for it.*

If an apology at the end of the lesson is forthcoming, you and the boy can move on. You've avoided an unnecessary confrontation. And the boy has learnt that you deal with these things reasonably and calmly.

Boys are often socialised to believe that aggression is the best way to deal with conflict. If we use appropriate alternatives, we not only reduce our own feelings of emotional exhaustion but also model more positive feelings for them to emulate. Through talking calmly to students about your frustration, and depersonalising things, you can clearly and politely re-frame your (often justifiable) fury as annoyance. Then the boys you teach are more likely to respect your feelings *and* improve their behaviour.

● **Display passion and enthusiasm during lessons**

Remember the research from earlier in the chapter that looked at the percentage of teachers who felt enjoyment, anger or anxiety while teaching? Well, further studies have found a positive relationship between teacher enjoyment and student outcomes. One study found that when lectures were performed with more enthusiasm it led to better test results.[30] Others have shown that teachers who enjoy learning help produce happy learners over time.[31] There's also a pedagogical element. As Frenzel et al. note:

> [Teacher]enjoyment has proven crucial not only for students' learning, performance, and well-being but also for teachers' classroom instruction and professional development.[32]

When you dislike teaching a class containing some difficult boys and the students pick up on it, this is what happens:

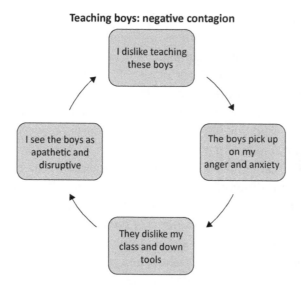

Teaching boys: negative contagion

When teachers feel a sense of excitement and enjoyment about teaching a class – especially ones containing boys who might be considered tricky characters – and they share this emotion with the class, the opposite happens. For example, with challenging classes I often say things like *Has anyone noticed that I didn't have to give out any warnings today? I love teaching this class when you're all doing the right things. And look at the standard of the work you've produced...*

Teaching boys: positive contagion

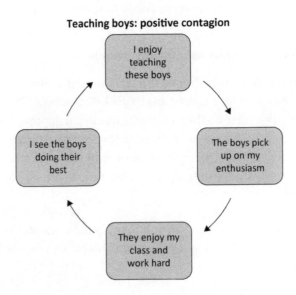

● **Be open about your motivation to teach**

Studies, such as Hassin et al. from 2005,[33] have demonstrated that humans spontaneously interpret the motives of others, especially when we have no obvious cues. Therefore, it's safe to assume that, even if we are guarded and closed about our background, students will inevitably make inferences about why we teach. I used to work in an all-boys comprehensive school in a very deprived inner-city area. I remember frequent grillings from the students about why I – a well-educated and ambitious person – had decided to switch from journalism, which they generally viewed as an enjoyable and high-status career, to teaching, which they mostly perceived as a terrible career, fit only for the inadequate or desperate. Also, why had I chosen to work in a lowly comp when, with my qualifications, I could surely have landed a role in a posh private school? I could have taken these questions as a slur on my career prospects or have seen them as intrusive incursions into my personal circumstances. Instead, I simply told them that I loved my subject, found teaching to be enjoyable and mentally stimulating, and thought that ensuring all students got the best possible education, including ones that don't live in fancy houses, was really important. Looking back now, I think my response led to them trusting my motives. They could tell that, no matter how annoying and frustrating they were at times, I really did enjoy teaching them all about prepositions and poetry.

• **Take care of your own mental health and work on subject knowledge weaknesses**

The classroom can be an exhausting environment at the best of times. But when we're feeling emotionally vulnerable, or are feeling that we're not doing a very good job, it can become a very difficult place to spend most of your working day. According to research by Hamre et al., teachers who felt depressed and had lower levels of self-efficacy generally reported 'more conflict with students in their classroom than expected based on levels of problem behaviours'.[34] In other words, conflict with boys in the classroom, even when we account for problematic behaviours, might also be heavily influenced by a teachers' state of mind and how confident they are in their ability to teach the subject.

The researchers found that some teachers regularly came into conflict with certain students 'despite low levels of teacher-reported problem behaviours'. These students managed to get on the nerves of their teachers without displaying particularly problematic behaviour.

This study fits the pattern of teachers tending to get annoyed and angry with boys because they see their behaviour as unacceptable. Often it is. But in other cases, they are unconsciously biased towards boys, disciplining them more for similar behaviour to girls[35] and, ultimately, contributing to, or even creating, the conflict that exists in classrooms in the first place. As the research suggests, it's not always problematic behaviour that drives teachers to vent their frustration with boys. In some cases, it's something more minor, but specific to how we feel about ourselves as educational professionals that pushes our buttons. While this may not be easy to accept or even acknowledge, it seems very unfair that when we feel fragile and are lacking confidence in our abilities, disadvantaged, 'low ability' boys seem to cop the most flak.

Behaviour tip 4: Subject knowledge is your suit of armour

When I stand in front of a class, really knowing my stuff makes me feel near invincible. Awkward questions, forceful challenges to my opinion, complaints about certain topics being boring: all of these bother me far less than they did when I was a fresh-faced NQT with subject-knowledge gaps. As we shall see in Chapter 5, some teachers become flustered and irritated by unwelcome questions that can lay bare their subject knowledge deficiencies. If you find yourself in this situation, rather than getting defensive and trying to bluster your way through things, depending on the context, use these responses:

• That's a really good question. Give me five minutes, I want to come back to you with a detailed answer

• That's an important question that we need to cover. Let's park it for now and we'll come back to it next lesson

- You know what, I'm not certain about the answer to that. Rather than giving you a rushed answer, I'm going to read up on that tonight and come back tomorrow with a proper response

- Mrs J. is an absolute expert on that topic. Let me speak to her at lunch and I'll see if she can nip in next lesson and talk you through it

As Hamre et al. assert 'teachers' self-efficacy may be a protective factor against the development of conflict'.[36] Or put more simply, the more confident you are in your ability to teach the subject, the greater likelihood of a harmonious environment where you and the boys you teach take mutual enjoyment in learning.

Staying cool

If you frequently get angry when teaching tricky boys (and girls), there are clear steps you can take to help protect you from a classroom full of conflict. First, take time before rushing into rash decisions. Second, avoid confrontation and communicate in a measured and professional way. Third, don't take things personally, but also avoid singling boys out. Fourth, work on areas that make you feel insecure when you're teaching certain lessons.

Finally, if you're still prone to bouts of anger, you might need to take further steps. Howard Kassinove – Professor Emeritus of Psychology at Hofstra University, and anger management expert – tells me that to reduce losses of temper, you need to 'take a *proactive* approach to working on anger. Eat well, sleep well, seek advice from trusted friends. If that does not work, professional counselling may be helpful.'

Staying cool in the face of a difficult class can take superhuman levels of patience. But taking deliberate steps to ensure that we deal with issues calmly and fairly is absolutely vital, for our own sakes, as well as for the outcomes of the boys we teach.

How should I react to boys who misbehave in my classroom?

STEPS TO SUCCESS

1 ADOPT
Adopt a direct but non-threatening manner

2 HEAT
Turn down the heat

3 RAISE
Raise the bar, not your voice

4 CONFLICT
Depersonalise conflict situations

5 PASSION
Show your passion and your knowledge

Notes

1 Johnson, S., Cooper, C., Cartwright, S., Donald, I., Taylor, P., & Millet, C. (2005) 'The experience of work-related stress across occupations', *Journal of Managerial Psychology*, 20:2, pp. 178–187.

2 Taxer, J.L., Becker-Kurz, B., & Frenzel, A.C. (2019) 'Do quality teacher–student relationships protect teachers from emotional exhaustion? The mediating role of enjoyment and anger', *Social Psychology of Education*, 22, pp. 209–226.

3 de Heus, P., & Diekstra, R.F.W. (1999) 'Do teachers burn out more easily? A comparison of teachers with other social professions on work stress and burnout symptoms', in R. Vandenberghe & A.M. Huberman (Eds.), *Understanding and Preventing Teacher Burnout: A Sourcebook of International Research and Practice* (pp. 269–284). New York: Cambridge University Press.

4 Hakanen, J.J., Bakker, A.B., & Schaufeli, W.B. (2006) 'Burnout and work engagement among teachers', *Journal of School Psychology*, 43:6, pp. 495–513.

5 See, for example, Fokkens-Bruinsma, M., & Canrinus, E. (2014) 'Motivation to become a teacher and engagement to the profession. Evidence from different contexts', *International Journal of Educational Research*, 65, pp. 65–74 and Watt, H.M.G., & Richardson, P.W. (2007) 'Motivational factors influencing teaching as a career choice: development and validation of the FIT-Choice Scale', *Journal of Experimental Education*, 75:3, pp. 167–202.

6 Butler, R. (2012) 'Striving to connect: extending an achievement goal approach to teacher motivation to include relational goals for teaching', *Journal of Educational Psychology*, 104:3, pp. 726–742.

7 Burić, I., Slišković, A., & Macuka, I. (2018) 'A mixed-method approach to the assessment of teachers' emotions: development and validation of the Teacher Emotion Questionnaire', *Educational Psychology*, 38:3, pp. 325–349.

8 Frenzel, A., Becker-Kurz, B., Pekrun, R., & Goetz, T. (2015) 'Teaching this class drives me nuts! - examining the person and context specificity of teacher emotions', *Plos One*, 10:6, pp. 1–15.

9 Burić, I., & Frenzel, A.C. (2019) 'Teacher anger: new empirical insights using a multi-method approach', *Teaching and Teacher Education*, 86, pp. 1–11.

10 See Chapter 5 for a detailed overview of this phenomenon.

11 Hamre, B., Pianta, R.C., Downer, J.T., & Mashburn, A.J. (2008) 'Teachers' perceptions of conflict with young students: looking beyond problem behaviours', *Social Development*, 17:1, pp. 115–136.

12 For evidence of this, Hamre et al. cite Bracken, B.A., & Craine, R.M. (1994) 'Children's and adolescents' interpersonal relations: do age, race, and gender define normalcy?', *Journal of Psychoeducational Assessment*, 12, pp. 14–32 and Ryan, R.M., Stiller, J.D., & Lynch, J.H. (1994) 'Representations of relationships to teachers, parents, and friends as predictors of academic motivation and self-esteem', *The Journal of Early Adolescence*, 14:2, pp. 226–249.

13 Hallam, S., & Parsons, S. (2012) 'Prevalence of streaming in UK primary schools: evidence from the Millennium Cohort Study', *British Educational Research Journal*, 39:3, pp. 514–544.

14 Taylor, B., Francis, B., Archer, L., Hodgen, J., Pepper, D., Tereshchenko, A., & Travers, M.-C. (2017) 'Factors deterring schools from mixed attainment teaching practice', *Pedagogy, Culture & Society*, 25:3, pp. 327–345.

15 See, for example, Ladd, G.W., Birch, S.H., & Buhs, E.S. (1999) 'Children's social and scholastic lives in kindergarten: related spheres of influence?' *Child development,* 70:6, pp. 1373–1400 and Murray, C., & Greenberg, M.T. (2000) 'Children's relationship with teachers and bonds with school. An investigation of patterns and correlates in middle childhood', *Journal of School Psychology,* 38:5, pp. 423–445.

16 Ibid.

17 Leung, D.Y.P., & Lee, W.W.S. (2006) 'Predicting intention to quit among Chinese teachers: differential predictability of the components of burnout', *Anxiety, Stress & Coping,* 19:2, pp. 129–141.

18 Klusmann, U., Kunter, M., Trautwein, U., Lüdtke, O., & Baumert, J. (2008b) 'Teachers' occupational well-being and quality of instruction: the important role of self-regulatory patterns', *Journal of Educational Psychology,* 100:3, pp. 702–715.

19 Sutton, R. (2007) 'Teachers' Anger, Frustration and Self-regulation', in Schultz, P.A., & Pekrun, R. (eds) *Emotion in Education* (pp. 259–274), Burlington, MA: Academic Press.

20 Farmer, T., Lines, M.M., & Hamm, J. (2011) 'Revealing the invisible hand: the role of teachers in children's peer experiences', *Journal of Applied Developmental Psychology,* 32, pp. 247–256.

21 Burgess, L.G., Riddell, P.M., Fancourt, A., & Murayama, K. (2018) 'The influence of social contagion within education: a motivational perspective', *Mind, Brain, and Education,* 12:4, pp. 164–174.

22 Oberle, E., & Schonert-Reichl, K.A. (2016) 'Stress contagion in the classroom? The link between classroom teacher burnout and morning cortisol in elementary school students', *Social Science and Medicine,* 159, pp. 30–37.

23 Such as Myers, S.A. (2002) 'Perceived aggressive instructor communication and student state motivation, learning, and satisfaction', *Communication Reports,* 15, pp. 113–121 and Wanzer, M.B., & McCroskey, J.C. (1998) 'Teacher socio-communicative style as a correlate of student affect toward teacher and course material', *Communication Education,* 47, pp. 43–52.

24 Boice, R. (1996) 'Classroom incivilities', *Research in Higher Education,* 37, pp. 453–486.

25 McPherson, M.B., & Young, S.L. (2004) 'What students think when teachers get upset: fundamental attribution error and student-generated reasons for teacher anger', *Communication Quarterly,* 52:4, pp. 357–369.

26 Guerrero, L.K. (1994) '"I'm so mad I could scream:" the effects of anger expression on relational satisfaction and communication competence', *Southern Communication Journal,* 59:2, pp. 125–141.

27 McPherson, M.B., Kearney, P., & Plax, T.G. (2003) 'The dark side of instruction: teacher anger as classroom norm violations', *Journal of Applied Communication Research,* 31:1, pp. 76–90.

28 Reid, K., Challoner, C., Lancet, A., Jones, G., Rhysiart, G.A., & Challoner, S. (2010) 'The views of primary school pupils at key stage 2 on school behaviour in Wales', *Educational Review,* 62:1, pp. 97–113.

29 This was a white lie, but there's nothing in the Teachers' Standards about minor fibs.

30 Ware, J. E., & Williams, R.G. (1975) 'The Dr. Fox effect: a study of lecturer effectiveness and ratings of instruction', *Journal of Medical Education,* 50:2, pp. 149–156.

31 Frenzel, A.C., Goetz, T., Lüdtke, O., Pekrun, R., & Sutton, R.E. (2009) 'Emotional transmission in the classroom: exploring the relationship between teacher and student enjoyment', *Journal of Educational Psychology,* 101:3, pp. 705–716.

32 Frenzel, A.C., Becker-Kurz, B., Pekrun, R., Goetz, T., & Lüdtke, O. (2018) 'Emotion transmission in the classroom revisited: a reciprocal effects model of teacher and student enjoyment', *Journal of Educational Psychology,* 110:5, pp. 628–639.

33 Hassin, R.R., Aarts, H., & Ferguson, M.J. (2005) 'Automatic goal inferences', *Journal of Experimental Social Psychology*, 41:2, pp. 129–140.
34 Ibid.
35 For a detailed summary of teacher bias and boys' behaviour, see Chapter 5 of Pinkett, M., & Roberts, M. (2019) *Boys Don't Try? Rethinking Masculinity in Schools*, Abingdon, Oxon: Routledge.
36 Ibid.

3 Do boys need male teachers as role models?

What's the issue?

You have a boy problem. You've seen all the statistics, especially the stark ones about working class boys. Negative attitudes to school work. Lower attainment levels. Greater involvement in crime and anti-social behaviour.

You're in charge of the education system. The gap between boys and girls is becoming a chasm. You need a solution. Why are so many of them doing so badly? What is holding them back? What are they lacking?

Then it hits you. Lots of these boys come from broken families. They are missing a man in their lives. A father figure. Someone to look up to. And when they go to school, they're taught by female teachers. That's it. That's the answer: these lads need male teachers to act as role models. That will be the thing that makes a difference...

The case for getting more men into teaching

Having an education system that mirrors the society we live in is, to my mind, an important aim. Seeing more men choosing teaching as an attractive career option would speak volumes about the sort of society we want to live in. This is particularly true of early years teaching. Think of the powerful impact of seeing larger numbers of men getting involved in the kind of nurturing role with which men have not been traditionally associated.

During our interview, Dr Simon Brownhill of Bristol University outlines some of the positives that increasing the number of male primary teachers would bring:

> Having male teachers reflects diversity and represents how school is a bubble of society. It makes it seem to be a good place to work to the students. It also breaks down stereotypes about gender by having teachers that are 'men who dare to care'. And, it's helpful to have male teachers who can act as mentors to male NQTs and help them cope with being in the minority. Finally, from

a parental perspective, fathers who may have had a negative experience of school may feel more comfortable stepping over the threshold to talk with a male teacher.

Furthermore, from a pastoral point of view, there are clear benefits to having more male primary teachers for older boys. McGrath and Sinclair's 2013 research asserts that boys are more likely to seek help from or confide in male primary teachers, especially when learning about and approaching puberty.[1]

Seeing more men in teaching roles, and especially in primary settings, would help change attitudes towards both education and society at large. It would probably encourage more boys to consider teaching as a possible future career option for themselves. But – and this is the key question that this chapter will address – would more male teachers make an actual differences to boys' attainment? Do male role model teachers inspire boys on to educational success?

The case for male teachers as role models

Simon Brownhill has focused much of his research on the male teacher role model debate, looking particularly at perceptions of male teachers of children aged 0–8. He tells me that during the 2000s, 'we saw a surge in government interest – particularly Western governments – in recruiting more men into the teaching profession, especially in the primary sector'.

According to Christine Skelton,[2] the perceived need for more male teachers as role models for boys emerged from a backdrop of societal unease about the issue of disaffected young males, especially those from lower socio-economic groups. Frequently, the narrative has switched between concerns about both white and black boys[3] from working-class backgrounds. David Cameron and Michael Gove both made speeches bemoaning the breakdown of traditional family structures and theorising that a positive male influence in the lives of boys, particularly those from single parent families, would help counter society's problems as well as boosting boys' educational achievement.

As Brownhill puts it, 'the theory went that male role models would ensure these youths had meaningful day-to-day contact with adults of the same gender and could help counter the feminisation of primary education by making schools "boy-friendly" again'.

An 'exodus' of male teachers?

Fast forward to 2020 and the male role model debate has been revisited, prompted by fears that boys are in danger of falling further behind educationally in the context of the pandemic. A report by the Education Policy Institute[4] argued that the proportion of men teaching in secondary schools has 'fallen steeply' over the last decade, while claiming that efforts to get more men into primary teaching have 'stagnated'. On initial reading, these are certainly worrying findings. Yet, on closer inspection, it transpires that the 'steep' fall in secondary male teachers equates to a relatively minor two percentage-point drop since 2010. Yet the two percentage-point rise in male primary teachers over the same period is curiously described as 'stagnating'. Predictably enough, imprecise language like this led to a raft of alarmist language from the print media, with *The Times* labelling the decline in male secondary teachers, with not a little hyperbole, as an 'exodus'.[5] Let's be clear – any discussion about male teachers leaving the profession is important. But sensationalist reporting about data detracts – and possibly distracts – from the most important question: why does teaching struggle to attract male recruits, especially when it involves teaching very young children?

Why are there so few male teachers in Early Years settings?

Recent research indicates that in England, just 2–3% of EYFS teachers are male. This figure follows the global average of 3%.[6] In his 2018 work, *Men in Early Years Settings*,[7] Brownhill identifies three main reasons why men are reluctant to get into teaching children aged 0–5:

1. Low pay

2. Status of the job

3. Fear of false child abuse allegations

During our interview, he points to other reasons why men are likely to eschew the idea of teaching the little ones:

> Teaching is hard work! That serves as a massive deterrent. Then there's the fear, as a lone male, of being isolated, of being part of what I call the 'gold dust gang'. As a year 1 teacher, I remember the only other man in the school being the janitor. We'd sit and chat, me talking about lesson plans and him telling me about cleaning fluid. Being a male primary school teacher – especially in the early years – acts as a challenge to your masculinity. Ultimately, there's a cultural perception that this is not 'man's work'. Claire Cameron[8] writes about the perception that men who work in primary schools must be (a) gay, (b) a paedophile or (c) a manager in waiting.

Listening to Brownhill talk about the reality for men working in early years, I'm struck by the challenges faced by the 3 percent. These men, it would seem are, at best, seen as curiosities or, at worst, as sexual deviants. It's understandable how men who might otherwise be tempted by a teaching career in the early years end up thinking it's not worth it, especially given the modest pay and stereotypical view that early years is all potato printing, wiping bums and not 'proper' teaching.

But, might these men be tempted into teaching by the idea of being a male role model? If the teacher training adverts explicitly called for more men to act as authentically masculine father figures, might that help recruit more men into the profession?

The teacher as substitute parent

Take a young boy without a father, give him the right kind of male teacher, and you'll turn him into a hard-working, driven and respectful young man. That's the idea behind the emphatic desire from politicians and other advocates for an increase in male teachers to act as role models for apparently rudderless young boys.

Yet, according to Brownhill, these 'common sense' calls for more male role models in early years teaching fall into the trap of blaming single parent families, often mothers, for gender attainment gaps:

> It plays to the notion that boys raised without a father have a deficient upbringing. Yet having a father can be a negative experience, as the present father might be absent much of the time, or uncaring, or abusive.

Furthermore, as Brownhill explains, the 'father figure' assumption misunderstands the fundamental difference between teaching and parenting a child:

> Caring and teaching are different roles. Am I meant to give them pocket money? The idea that we should have male teachers serving as surrogate dads is one that I strongly contest. As a young teacher, I wasn't ready, willing or able to take on that burden. I was focused on trying to learn my craft. I'm expected to be a teacher *and* a dad? How can you manage to merge these two roles?

The male role model teacher: A job description

Sycamore Grove Primary School – Male NQT teacher for EYFS

We are seeking to recruit an inspirational male teacher, who will embody the school's values of respect, reliability and trustworthiness, as we take the next step on our journey towards becoming an Outstanding provider of education. Popular with all colleagues, parents and children, the successful candidate will be kind, creative, emotionally intelligent, approachable, a good listener, calm at all times, possess excellent behaviour management skills, have a great sense of humour and be highly adept at delivering each aspect of the curriculum. As a keen sportsman with a passion for coaching teams, he will exude physical strength and, as such, will be expected to lead on outdoor learning activities.

The above advertisement isn't real. But despite being a spoof, it gives a flavour of the bewildering array of characteristics expected of a male teacher earmarked as a male role model.

In a key 2008 study, Penni Cushman surveyed 250 New Zealand primary school principals to discover how they defined the male role model and what qualities they were seeking in male teachers who might take on that role.[9] A massive 87% of female principals and 94% of male principals stated that the education system needed more male role models. And their reasons for this belief?

The main reason principals gave for needing more male role models was to meet the needs of children from single-parent families. The second most cited reason... was to provide sports leadership.

In a country obsessed with rugby, it is disappointing but perhaps not surprising that school leaders placed a higher value on a potential male teacher's sporting prowess than his academic background:

> The number of references among the principals' responses to sporting attributes far outweighed those to learning and achievement.

These views were shared by some of the female principals who, when faced with candidates who didn't meet the typical rugby-playing mould, reverted to homophobic caricature:

> Recently we had two positions going in our school. We interviewed males for each. To be honest they appeared ineffectual and woosy. Their handshakes were limp and they were not what I would call male role models. We employed two efficient, strong females.

As I discussed in Chapter 7 of *Boys Don't Try?*, the quest for strong, sporty, authoritarian role models risks perpetuating traditional forms of masculinity, which see academic work as the province of girls and effeminate boys. As Wayne Martino puts it, worrying that primary education has become overly-feminised and therefore attempting to recruit certain types of men into teaching, results in the role model becoming 'synonymous with being a 'real man' who is able to ensure that boys' masculinity remains intact or is appropriately cultivated'.[10]

Indeed, when we dig a little deeper into Cushman's research, we see that gender stereotypes play a much smaller part in the average principal's role model wish list than first appears. Cushman revealed that 'the qualities just over a half of the principals look for in a male "role model" are the same qualities that they look for in any teacher'. These findings mirror the results of research into student perceptions of male role models. For example, Elina Lahelma found that Finnish students aged 13–14 didn't care about the gender of their teachers.[11] Instead of a fixed view of an inspirational male figure, they appreciated 'teachers, irrespective of gender, who can teach and are friendly and relaxed, but who nevertheless keep order and make sure that students work'.

Look back again at my person specification. Is any one man capable of being all those things, all the time, to all stakeholders?

As Simon Brownhill asserts in his ironically-titled research paper 'Build me a male role model!':[12]

> No two male role models are likely to be the same, particularly when one considers how different contexts, situations and expectations are likely to seek different requirements of the male role model.

In other words, politicians, headteachers, governors, parents and children all want different things from a male role model. And often, they don't even know what they want. Brownhill's research threw up over 65 desirable characteristics. How can one man, he asks during our interview, be expected to emulate all these personality types? It would appear that proponents of the male role model theory have a vague sense that boys need fixing and that parachuting in an incoherently-defined, all-things-to-all-men man will somehow magically narrow the attainment gap.

Do children view teachers as role models?

Even if teachers were willing to try and adopt the position of father figure, there's little evidence to suggest that boys would see them as a substitute parents. On a wider level, *children simply don't see teachers as role models*. During our conversation, Brownhill explains that very young children find it difficult to understand the concept of role models, let alone the teacher as role model:

> Consider KS1 children for example. They might idolise cartoon characters or images from picture books, or uncles or the local bus driver. Children look up to those who are generationally, geographically and experientially close to their lives: older siblings, near peers and so on.

It might be difficult for adults to grasp that a young boy reveres a fictional character like George Pig more than his teacher Mr Jenkins. Or to accept that, despite spending several hours a day in Mr Jenkins' classroom, he is more likely to ape the behaviour of his raspberry-blowing older sister, or that funny lad who lives two doors down from his house. But this is the reality of young boys' lives.

Is it an age thing?

But what about older children? Are teenagers, for example, more impressed by teachers than younger children? Research by Patricia Bricheno and Mary Thornton found a diverse range of role models inspiring their sample of 379 children aged 10–16.[13] They noted that 'both girls and boys named relatives as most important role models more often than they named anyone else'. Friends also played a prominent part in the students' responses. By stark contrast, teachers barely got a look-in.

Bricheno and Thornton state that 'very few teachers were named' as role models by boys or girls. Compared to 32% of young people who looked up to a parent as a role model, only a paltry 2.4% of pupils in the study identified a teacher as a role model. Like Brownhill, Ashley (2003) also argues that popular members of their peer group, rather than teachers, are boys' main role models.[14] And yet research consistently shows that teachers buy into the role model theory. Research by de Salis et al., for example, found that 80% of male (and 60% of female) trainee teachers felt 'that all boys needed a male teacher role model…and that boys without a father at home needed a male teacher role model'.[15]

Why are teachers misled into believing that they can be role models? Perhaps it's because when they were at school – largely well-behaved, apple-fetching mini-pedagogues in the making – they were the tiny percentage who looked up to their teachers.

When it comes to teachers, kids will often like them. They'll also feel grateful for their support and guidance. They might even hold them in high esteem. But that's about as far as it goes. For advocates of a 'male teacher role model' programme, this is a very inconvenient and overlooked fact.

Do boys learn better with male teachers?

A central justification of the need for more male role models has been the belief that disaffected boys will respond better to teachers of their own gender. Boys who don't like reading, for example, who might not have dads at home to read them a bedtime story; by giving these boys a same-sex role model as a teacher, you'll provide a man to emulate, resulting in an improvement to their literacy and enthusiasm for reading.

A 2010 study by Lam et al. of nearly 5,000 Grade 4 students in Hong Kong saw *no* evidence that boys improved their reading when taught by men. In fact, their results found that 'both boys and girls learnt better when taught by women'.[16] In 2008, Carrington et al. found no teacher gender effect on attainment data and pupil attitudes in British primary schools.[17] In the same year, Marsh et al. found 'little or no evidence' to support the idea that boys will be more motivated by male than female teachers in secondary maths, science and English classes.[18] An international review on gender and education from 2007 indicated that 'the gender of teachers has little, if any, effect on the achievement of pupils',[19] while in 2013, Geri Smyth of the University of Strathclyde stated that 'no studies have indicated improved achievement of pupils (regardless of stage, age, ethnicity or social class) where their gender was matched with that of their teachers'.[20]

So, to summarise, the idea of the male teacher as role model is deeply problematic for the following reasons:

1. Unless pay and conditions improve, and societal attitudes towards primary school teaching change, we are unlikely to be able to recruit enough men to fit the role

2. Children very rarely view teachers as role models

3. Nobody can agree on the desirable qualities of the ideal male role model anyway

4. Male role models are often expected to embody the potentially harmful 'real man' stereotype

5. Male teachers aren't able to act as surrogate parents

6. There is very little evidence that placing male teachers with male pupils improves their academic performance or attitudes to learning

Given this compelling list, should we just abandon the idea of the male role model altogether? Or are there other benefits to having male teachers teaching boys? And, if so, what can teachers and school leaders do to harness the idea for positive gain?

What can we do about it?

If you're keen to try and push boys to greater academic success, I'd recommend doing the following:

● **Stop talking about 'role models'**

As we've seen, even if the evidence was in favour of male role models lifting boys' attainment (it isn't, of course), then the mantle of the male role model is enough to suffocate any enthusiastic new male entrant to the profession.

For this reason, Simon Brownhill recommends abandoning the term altogether:

It's time for those working in education to move away from the term 'role model'. Instead, we should use the term 'facilitator'. As a facilitator, a teacher can signpost children towards positive influences, whether that's in books, on television, YouTube, or in the community. These influences would be things, people, experiences and ideas that develop their interests and understanding.[21]

The shift in language is more than semantic. In recognising the limitations of our knowledge, experiences and personal attributes, as *facilitators* we can be far more realistic about what we can do collectively, rather than individually, to meet the needs, and develop the powerful knowledge, of the boys we teach.

● **Be yourself**

When I visit schools, I'm frequently asked the same question by female teachers of boys: what can I do to be an effective role model to boys? As the evidence has shown, the narrative of the heroic male role model come to rescue the boys – particularly primary school boys – from the feminised world of school, and the 'deficit' of having a single mum parent, is deeply flawed. So it's tempting to respond: *carry on doing what you're doing.* But a better answer still might be: *be yourself.* As Brownhill notes:

> Being who you are is really important. Children don't look to just one person as a role model. A role model is not encapsulated in one person. It's an amalgamation of different people and different states, a swirl of experiences and ideas that create this mythical person. The assertion that one man – or indeed woman – can do everything to inspire a young person is completely wrong.

With that in mind, it's important to see yourself as someone who can play a contributory role in young boys' lives, and someone whose efforts and behaviours boys would wish to emulate. And the best way to make any kind of mark is to be kind, teach well, but be willing to hold them to account – calmly – when their effort or behaviour fall below the standard you expect.

Many aeons ago, I was a young NQT in a tough boys' school. We went to the pub after my first week of teaching. I remember one of the behaviour mentors – a muscular bloke who seemed to be permanently clad in motorbike leathers – telling me that, like him, I should take up bodybuilding in order to gain the boys' respect. Thankfully, I managed to resist the allure of kettle bells, protein shakes and ill-fitting spandex vests, and decided to just be me instead.

● **Avoid being pigeonholed**

Against their better judgement, teachers are often encouraged to adopt a persona based on a school's expectations of them. These expectations tend to derive from assumptions based on specific stereotypes, usually based on the teacher's gender, ethnicity or social class. As DeMarco Ryans' concerning but ultimately uplifting case study illustrates, attempting to meet unwelcome and often prejudicial expectations can lead to feelings of self-doubt and painful questions about your personal and professional identity:

CASE STUDY

DeMarco Ryans, English teacher and head of literacy

Talk to a teacher for long enough and the word 'expectation' will find its way into the conversation. More often than not, when teachers talk about expectations, they are talking about behaviour.

As professionals, we also have a prominent set of expectations. Built around providing excellent outcomes for students, the Teachers' Standards provide us with a road map for best practice that can be repeated in any setting around the nation.

However, when it comes to how teachers make progress and what they progress in, expectations are not universal but underpinned by attitudes and conventions that are intrinsic to a respective school's culture, or in the values of individual line managers. As we shall see from my experiences at three different schools, these expectations can empower or disenfranchise a teacher.

School A, is an academy located in the borough of Merton, graded by OFSTED as 'Good', having transformed from the 'Inadequate' label. My first, much anticipated, contact with the school was on a tour as a member of the 2015 Teach First English cohort. I had not anticipated that this would be my first encounter with the type of pervasive thinking that has maligned the development of primarily Black and Asian teachers: that we excel at being 'role models' and 'behaviour managers'.

I can't recall my would-be professional mentor's words verbatim. But having known me for less than an hour, she proclaimed my value to the school would be my ability to be a role model to its Black boys. This was because like many of them, I was Black, and unlike the existing Black teachers at the school who were from Africa and the Caribbean – the wrong kind of Black – I was Black *and British*, and consequently better equipped to lead these young men into their coming of age. Critiquing her rationale is for another text at another time. Instead I want to use this as an example of how uninvited and unwarranted expectations can impose on the autonomy of new or young teachers in determining *why* they teach.

Rather than thinking about what I taught and how I taught it, my confidence was undermined with thoughts of, 'do they see me as some glorified youth worker?'. Other members of staff repeated this sentiment during the early months of my placement. My subject knowledge and ability to teach appeared to be third or fourth in importance, below the perception that I had some ability that allowed me to speak to 'those boys'. I found myself prioritising being their pastoral carer rather than their educator. I struggled to get the balance right and came under criticism from my mentors for the stagnation of my pedagogy. My planning became uncertain and my instruction lacked conviction. This experience left me demoralised and doubting whether I had the intelligence and ability to be an effective teacher. That uncertainty clung to me until February 2016 when I visited School C during a week's placement. My experience there was so liberating that I returned to School A an independent practitioner. I no longer felt I needed to be a role model in order to teach. For me, it was enough that my teaching made me a strong classroom and community presence and thus a better professional.

I moved to **School B**, on the outskirts of Guildford, at the start of my NQT year in 2016. Celebrated as an 'Outstanding' school and teaching hub for the local area, I felt that in this environment I would begin to shape my professional identity outside of my classroom identity.

In the spring of my NQT year, I was asked by the Headteacher to interview for a behaviour management role. The interview process helped me better understand some of the expectations of middle leaders but I chose to withdraw on the basis that the opportunity and my development as an NQT were not aligned. At the start of the subsequent academic year, the conversation resurfaced following the launch of a behaviour and inclusion unit. The Head felt that my presence and personality were well-suited to working with boys who would otherwise face external exclusions. I do build effective relationships with young people who acquire the 'challenging' student label, but this is an aspect of my practice with all students, and this attribute is about much more than my ethnicity, my build or my personality. Once again, the pernicious perception that my value was rooted in management of 'the other' began to take shape.

In the summer term, sensing that this would forever be my position, I applied for a role at another local school. I was upfront with my Head and my colleagues about my interest in this school, which was new and presented the opportunity to invest in a culture still forming.

The Head of the prospective school extended a subject teacher job offer with extra responsibilities that aligned with my personal vision for pastoral support. I arranged to meet with my Head at School B, since I had agreed to keep them informed before making my final decision. After I outlined the opportunity presented to me and the reasons for its appeal, I asked one sincere question, 'Do you have a vision of what you see as my future at this school?'

The ensuing response? I was chastised and called an opportunist, unappreciative and selfish. I was warned that moving school for a second time in my three-year career would reflect poorly on my CV. The nail in the coffin was being told I needed to be loyal, unmotivated by money, and see a few more classes through. The meeting ended. I was stunned. Was my Head right? Had I overestimated my abilities? Was this about money, not an opportunity to contribute in ways that allowed me agency? Was I committing the sin of choosing myself above my school? If the Head's intention was to shatter my confidence and render me afraid to take a leap of faith in myself, thereby remaining at the school that year, it worked. I stayed.

Located in Woking, I was offered a job at **School C** in December 2018 and began in September 2019. A Catholic school that routinely appears among the top twenty state schools in the country, School C prides itself on sustaining and advancing the learning experience of its students and staff.

Truthfully, School C is a living example of an adage that I heard from a speaker at an INSET I attended in my final months at School B, 'A good school trains its staff well enough that they could leave, but it treats them well enough that they don't want to.' School C's approach to staff development is focused on the individual. Our professional development portfolios are built on our individual ambitions and interests, affording us a more personal level of investment. Those of us in middle leadership roles are supported through training programmes to define and refine what this means to us and how we deliver our roles by optimising our abilities and serving the school's priorities. Our Head seeks out staff for their advice and perspectives on their career progression, resulting in an awareness that allows him to support the direction his colleagues are moving in. The consequence of this staff development infrastructure is a faculty of well-trained staff, confident in their abilities and authentic in their nature. Yes, each year some teachers are prepared and ready to leave, but many more stay and continue to enrich the quality of the school to the benefit of our students.

A few months after joining School C's faculty, I was encouraged to interview for Head of Literacy. The school was aware of my interest in raising standards in pupil attainment and they felt that the combination of my research-focused practice, subject knowledge and expertise as an English Teacher would make me an ideal candidate.

> Unlike my earlier painful experiences, questions about how my development could contribute to the growth of the school were made in partnership with me. At long last, following my appointment, I had a genuine sense of agency about my work and my professional identity.

● Don't expect all male (and female) teachers to be alike

The assumption that men are ideally placed to deal with behaviour isn't just an example of stereotypical pigeonholing. It also fails to appreciate the nurturing potential of male teachers. A recent Austrian observational study[22] found, for example, that a large majority of boys aged 4–6 were drawn towards male educators, seeking 'need for security', 'support with exploration' and 'joy in physical contact'. The researchers acknowledge that the boys' desire for physical proximity might be explained by the male teachers' scarcity, which lends them an appealing 'exotic status'. Interestingly, the researchers found that these male teachers didn't fit the stereotypical view of the male teacher as the disciplinarian, ready to solve society's ills by dealing with unruly boys. On the contrary, they were 'less… "punitive" and significantly more yielding, appearing to practise a "relaxed" approach.' We shouldn't, however, be surprised by these findings. As Becky Francis has previously made clear, it is ridiculous to expect that male teachers all teach alike, based on their shared experience of 'maleness'. Indeed, a 2018 study into the language used by UK and German teachers:

> found no discernible difference between the genders in the range of strategies used. Both male and female teachers shifted between strategies traditionally viewed as masculine and feminine. The key influencing factor affecting linguistic choices appeared to be the culture of the workplace and not gender.[23]

Our views and expectations of our teachers should not be defined by their gender. Within classrooms, staff rooms, HR departments and SLT meeting rooms, we need to challenge stereotypical views about the characteristics of male and female teachers. If you're worried that behaviour is slipping in your school, don't just employ a big guy with a gruff voice. Work on improving the culture of the school by empowering and supporting each member of staff to instil clear routines and boundaries. If you want to create a more nurturing environment, hire people who will develop excellent, caring relationships with students, regardless of their mixture of chromosomes.

No more role models

Having decided to reject the burdensome and ineffective role model label, we need to consider an alternative model for inspiring and enabling boys to succeed. Here's what I think it should look like in your classroom:

| Identify | Empathise | Facilitate | Reflect |

Identify   What's holding this boy back? Is it basic literacy skills? Are there issues at home that require further pastoral support? Is peer pressure making him feel unable to try his hardest in front of other boys? Is there a particular lesson that he loves? What can I learn from that?

Empathise   What steps can I take to show this boy that I care about both his personal growth and his academic progress? How does he respond to his peers and adults? What is most likely to motivate him to succeed?

Facilitate   Are my knowledge and skills sufficient to address his academic and pastoral needs? What resources and methods can I use/adapt/direct him to in order to inspire him to learn more effectively?

Reflect   How effective have my efforts been? What progress has he made following my interventions? Have I identified the issues correctly? Have I built a relationship built on trust and challenge? What more can I, or others, do to encourage him to strive for excellence?

● Get men into teaching for the right reasons

This chapter has been focused on debunking the male role model theory. Despite the lack of evidence for the claim that more men will improve boys' attainment or attitudes to learning, as was stated at the outset, I still believe that getting more men into teaching, particular in early years settings, is a laudable and sensible aim.

Ultimately, while male teachers can't operate effectively as role models, having them in a nursery or reception class – or indeed in a year 10 GCSE Dance class – speaks volumes in itself about the kind of society we want our students to see. As long as we can cast aside the damaging notion of the firm-handshaked, sport-loving macho man, seeing more men adopting caring, nurturing roles, while being excellent teachers in their own right, sends out important signals to boys about what kind of person they might want to be when they grow up.

Do boys need male teachers as role models?

Notes

1 McGrath, K., & Sinclair, M. (2013) 'More male primary-school teachers? Social benefits for boys and girls', *Gender and Education*, 25:5, pp. 531–547.
2 Skelton, C. (2009) 'Failing to get men into primary teaching: a feminist critique', *Journal of Education Policy*, 24:1, pp. 39–54.
3 See Maylor, U. (2009) 'They do not relate to Black people like us': Black teachers as role models for Black pupils, *Journal of Education Policy*, 24:1, pp. 1–21 for a detailed overview of the evidence for this argument.
4 Education Policy Institute. (2020) *Trends in the diversity of teachers in England*, Education Policy Institute. Available at: https://epi.org.uk/publications-and-research/diversity-of-teachers/ (Accessed 24th October 2020).
5 Hurst, G. (2020) 'Exodus of male teachers leaves boys without role models', The Times, 19th October 2020. Available at: https://www.thetimes.co.uk/article/exodus-of-male-teachers-leaves-boys-without-role-models-xdkstxj9r#:~:text=The%20exodus%20over%20the%20past,in%20seven%20teachers%20is%20male (Accessed 24th October 2020).
6 Warin, J. (2019) 'Conceptualising the value of male practitioners in early childhood education and care (ECEC): gender balance or gender flexibility', *Gender and Education*, 31:3, pp. 293–308.
7 Brownhill, S., & Wright, D. (2018) *Men in Early Years Settings*, London: Jessica Kingsley Publishers.
8 Cameron, C., Moss, P., & Owen, C. (1999) *Men in the Nursery*, London: Sage.
9 Cushman, P. (2008) 'So what exactly do you want? What principals mean when they say 'male role model'', *Gender and Education*, 20:2, pp. 123–136.
10 Martino, W. (2008) 'Male teachers as role models: addressing issues of masculinity, pedagogy and the re-masculinization of schooling', *Curriculum Inquiry*, 38:2, pp. 189–223.
11 Lahelma, E. (2000) 'Lack of male teachers: a problem for students or teachers?' *Pedagogy, Culture and Society*, 8, pp. 173–186.
12 Brownhill, S. (2014) ''Build me a male role model!' A critical exploration of the perceived qualities/characteristics of men in the early years (0–8) in England', *Gender and Education*, 26:3, pp. 246–261.
13 Bricheno, P., & Thornton, M. (2007) 'Role model, hero or champion? Children's views concerning role models', *Educational Research*, 49:4, pp. 383–396.
14 Ashley, M. (2003) 'Primary school boys' identity formation and the male role model: an exploration of sexual identity and gender identity in the UK through attachment theory', *Sex Education*, 3:3, pp. 257–270.
15 de Salis, C.A., Rowley, A., Stokell. K., & Brundrett, M. (2019) 'Do we need more male primary teachers? Tensions and contradictions in the perspectives of male and female trainees', *Education 3–13*, 47:4, pp. 475–489 and Wood, P., & Brownhill, S. (2018) ''Absent fathers', and children's social and emotional learning: an exploration of the perceptions of 'positive male role models' in the primary school sector', *Gender and Education*, 30:2, pp. 172–186.
16 Lam, Y.H., Tse, S.K., Lam, J.W.I., & Loh, K.Y.E. (2010) 'Does the gender of the teacher matter in the teaching of reading literacy? Teacher gender and pupil attainment in reading literacy in Hong Kong', *Teaching and Teacher Education*, 26, pp. 754–759.
17 Carrington, B., Tymms, P., & Merrell, C. (2008) 'Role models, school improvement and the 'gender gap' - Do men bring out the best in boys and women the best in girls?' *British Educational Research Journal*, 34, pp. 315–327.

18 Marsh, H., Martin, A., & Cheng, J. (2008) 'A multilevel perspective on gender in class-room motivation and climate: potential benefits of male teachers for boys?' *Journal of Educational Psychology*, 100, pp. 78–95.

19 Sabbe, E., & Aelterman, A. (2007) 'Gender in teaching: a literature review', *Teachers and Teaching: Theory and Practice,* 13:5, pp. 521–538 cited in de Salis, C.A., Rowley, A., Stokell. K., & Brundrett, M. (2019) 'Do we need more male primary teachers? Tensions and contradictions in the perspectives of male and female trainees', *Education 3–13*, 47:4, pp. 475–489.

20 Cited in Hepburn, H. (2013) 'Revealed: tales of the anxious males on primary's front line', *The Times Educational Supplement Scotland*, London, Issue. 2304, (Feb 15, 2013)

21 For more on this idea, see Brownhill, S., Warwick, P., Warwick, J., & Brown-Hajdukova, E. (2020) "Role model' or 'facilitator'? Exploring male teachers' and male trainees' perceptions of the term 'role model' in England', *Gender and Education*, pp. 1–16.

22 Huber, J., & Traxl, B. (2018) 'Pedagogical differences and similarities between male and female educators, and their impact on boys' and girls' behaviour in early childhood education and care institutions in Austria', *Research Papers in Education*, 33:4, pp. 452–471.

23 McDowell, J., & Klattenberg, R. (2019) 'Does gender matter? A cross-national investigation of primary class-room discipline', *Gender and Education*, 31:8, pp. 947–965, cited in de Salis, C.A., Rowley, A., Stokell. K., & Brundrett, M. (2019) 'Do we need more male primary teachers? Tensions and contradictions in the perspectives of male and female trainees', *Education 3–13*, 47:4, pp. 475–489.

PART B
Instilling high expectations in boys

4 How can I improve the study skills of the boys I teach?

What's the issue?

Let's begin with an uncomfortable truth: no matter how good the teaching, once our students leave the classroom, their performance could well be undermined by poor study behaviours. In their 2008 meta-analysis of over 70,000 students in the United States, Crede and Kuncel concluded that students' study habits, skills and attitudes 'were found to rival standardized tests and previous grades as predictors of academic performance'.[1]

What do we mean by study skills, habits and attitudes?

In their helpful summary of teaching study skills Fisher and Frey (2017) break the term down into three wide-ranging but essential areas:[2]

1. Cognitive skills – including note-taking, mnemonics, mind-mapping and flash cards.

2. Metacognitive skills – such as planning, monitoring, time managing, rehearsing and self-evaluation.

3. Affective skills – this term covers overlapping concepts like motivation, agency and self-concept. These are the kind of skills that we covered in detail in Chapter 1.

The effectiveness of our students' study skills will have a big impact on their academic outcomes. A student who can appreciate not only which revision techniques to use (cognitive skill) but also understand when to adapt and refine the use of these techniques (metacognitive skill) has a far better chance of success than one who plods on through their notes robotically.

Teachers try their best to close attainment gaps during lessons. But what if our students are hampering their efforts to memorise knowledge, by sticking to familiar but flawed study techniques, like a teenager clutching on to a comforting but tattered childhood toy?

There's a significant body of research that suggests that certain study methods better help students retain and recall key knowledge. But how confident can we be that our students – especially the underperforming boys – are embracing these vital techniques?

Which study techniques are ineffective?

In an important 2013 study, Dunlosky et al.[3] evaluated the effectiveness of ten learning strategies that are popular with students. They argued that some of the most frequently used study techniques have a 'low utility level' and should be avoided. Other techniques were assigned a 'high utility level', given the wealth of research supporting their effectiveness as study tools:

Effectiveness	Technique	Explanation
Low utility ✘	Rereading notes, textbooks, revision guides etc.	• Gives students a shallow understanding of what they have read • Any benefits tend to be short-term in nature • Can often remember things shortly after rereading but struggle with long-term recall and comprehension
Low utility ✘	Highlighting	• Gives students an illusion of fluency yet offers little long-term cognitive benefit • Students usually mark too much text when highlighting, so key information is less likely to be remembered • Novices find picking out the main points of a topic difficult • Students who use highlighters during tests only perform at a similar level as those who have merely read the text
High utility ✓	Retrieval practice	• Using aids like flashcards forces students to recall information from memory • Makes students face up to the gaps in their knowledge • Offers clear advantages in follow-up assessments

Effectiveness	Technique	Explanation
High utility ✓	Spaced practice	• Encourages students to distribute their revision in smaller chunks over a longer period of time • Ensures they revisit things they haven't recently learned • Students who space their revision outperform those who study by cramming in long sessions just before a test

Using retrieval practice and spaced practice feels significantly more challenging than rereading or highlighting notes, which feel good but don't really work. By emphasising the usefulness of the power of retrieval and spaced practice, Dunlosky et al. contend, teachers can help underperforming students maximise their potential.

Is retrieval practice useful for younger children?

Reading research into the most effective study techniques, we might be forgiven for picturing them being used by older students, hunched over desks, late at night, ahead of GCSE, A level and degree examinations. Yet studies have shown that younger children also benefit when using these strategies. For example, Dunlosky et al.[4] point to research which found learning advantages in the use of spaced practice for nursery children, who could recall more visual detail over time.[5] Karpicke et al. (2016) found that 9–11-year olds made learning gains from retrieval practice in terms of recall and item recognition.[6] While some studies suggest that the benefits of retrieval are relatively greater with slightly older children[7] – the age of 8 is mentioned in this research – Dunlosky et al.'s overview[8] details a deep body of research, which allows them to conclude that 'some form of testing effect [i.e. positive impact of retrieval practice] has been demonstrated' with EYFS, primary school and middle school children. Researchers into psychology and cognitive science may quibble over the precise advantages of retrieval and spaced practice for children of different ages, but there appears to be a consensus that they will all benefit in some way from frequent low-stakes testing.

Do students use the most effective study strategies?

In his recent overview of improving learning and memory,[9] Jeffrey Karpicke notes that 'many learners do not practice retrieval as often or as effectively as they could'. Despite the very limited usefulness of rereading notes and textbooks, Karpicke et al. found that even when students were made aware of the cognitive benefits of retrieval practice and the negatives associated with rereading, they still made poor metacognitive choices: 'not only was repetitive reading the most frequently listed strategy, it was also the strategy most often listed as students' number one choice, by a large margin'.[10]

Students' awareness of their unsatisfactory study effort were also in evidence in a 2013 study by Susser and McCabe, who found that students tend to dedicate less time studying for a particular topic than they themselves believe should be undertaken by a typical 'good student'.[11] Put simply, despite knowing the effort that is required to get good grades, many students still don't live up to this standard, even though they realise this means they'll not meet their potential.

Blaisman et al.'s 2017 research compared students' study skills intentions to their actual study habits. They discovered that, ahead of looming exams, students professed that they intended to follow good study practices and 'intended to rely more heavily on flashcards and taking practice tests'. Yet, in reality, their best-laid plans soon went awry and these 'two strategies ended up being two of the most infrequently used'.[12] Cramming was a popular strategy, used by the majority of students, who despite what we know about the benefits of spaced practice, largely began studying 'about two days before the exam', with '53% admitting to studying in a single session right before an exam'. Perhaps most perturbing of all is the paltry number of hours students spent studying in total for each exam. Taking their own research and past studies into account, Blaisman et al. calculate that 'the majority of students study about four hours total per exam'. Yes, I'm afraid you did read that right: *four hours* in total *per exam*.

Even when students have an awareness of the most effective learning strategies, they often forget or become confused about the relative strengths of different learning strategies. Blaisman et al. give the example of some students asserting that rereading textbooks was an ineffective strategy but erroneously believing that rereading notes was somehow more effective. Their confusion is unsurprising and understandable, however, when we take into account the mixed messages about study skills coming from teachers. A 2015 study by Morehead et al.,[13] for example, worryingly found that 41% of teachers recommended that their students should use rereading when studying.

How does gender influence study skills?

The studies we've looked at so far, though very insightful, view students as a homogenous lump. Given the concerning evidence about the sloppy and unhelpful study habits of the student population as a whole, how might things look when we take gender into account? Might it be that boys are particularly prone to the lure of ineffective study skills?

Blaisman et al. didn't investigate gender differences in their study. Yet they put forward a couple of interesting reasons for why students might fail to use the most beneficial study strategies:

1. They don't know how to study effectively

2. They do but having left things too late, they abandon the most effective study skills and fall back on easy but ineffective strategies

As someone who bangs on relentlessly to students about the cognitive advantages of retrieval practice and spaced practice, reading this, I couldn't help but think about the many boys who I've taught who ended up fitting the description of the second scenario.

But, beyond my anecdotal hunch, is there any evidence that boys are more likely to fall behind with their revision and then hinder their progress by reverting back to less useful study skills?

Boys' study habits: The grim truth

Teachers who are working hard to boost the grades of their underperforming male students may need to brace themselves. The research into boys' study skills makes for very grim reading. As Ronnel B. King illustrates,[14] boys:

- start their homework later in the day than girls[15] and spend less time completing it (nearly half the time spent by girls in some studies)[16]

- are more likely than girls to come to school unprepared[17]

- are less likely than girls to seek help from others with academic work, even when they are struggling or stuck[18]

- are less likely than girls to make plans, and monitor their thoughts during study[19]

- are far less likely than girls to set themselves up in a helpful environment and consider time allocations for different homework tasks[20]

- work slowly, inconsistently and produce scruffier work that is poorly planned and lacking in detail[21]

I could go on.

Why are so many boys reluctant to study at home?

Why do so many of them cower at the sight of a revision timetable, like Superman shrinking back from a glowing green hunk of Kryptonite? Peer pressure, which enforces stereotypical ideas that scholarly dedication is a feminine trait, undoubtedly plays a central role in this approach.[22] Yet attitudes at home also contribute towards many boys' unwillingness to launch themselves into home learning. According to Harris et al.,[23] this gender difference can be explained by the practices in the homes and communities where boys live where, traditionally, men attempt to keep a distinct separation between time spent at work and time spent at home avoiding work. By contrast, women are seen as the organisers, juggling full or part-time work with planning for domestic tasks and managing the household's relations with the outside world. For Harris et al., this traditional 'regime' is replicated in the way that the two genders approach homework: girls are largely organised and ready to deal with the challenge of homework, whereas boys are reluctant to blur the boundary between school (work) and home (relaxation and play).

It would appear then, that some boys are socialised to see homework as an unwelcome addition to their home life, an intrusive burden that eats into their social time, which therefore must be navigated quickly and without much effort. Like a visit by Uncle Jeff but with a focus on algebra instead of racist jokes.

But what about those golden study strategies? The ones identified by Dunlosky et al. as the most effective study techniques. Can we at least console ourselves with some evidence that boys are studying smartly, even if they aren't as dedicated to their homework as the girls?

Boys and the most effective study skills

Unfortunately, according to the research, the answer appears to be 'no'. A recent study of 1,371 Canadian undergraduates suggests that females are more likely to engage in spaced learning than their male peers.[24] A notable study by Griffin et al., which identified a strong correlation between a student's study skills and academic success, found a statistically significant difference in these skills between male and female students.[25] They argued that:

> The primary conclusion from this study is that contrary to prior research that suggests that females predominantly outperform males in academics, such differences can be better explained by mediating variables such as learning and study strategies.

In other words, when the researchers controlled for these study skills, the male and female attainment gap disappeared. Let's just pause for a second and take in this finding. Yes, it's just one study, but the conclusion – that gender gaps are largely down to boys' inferior study skills – could have seismic implications for those of us who are kept awake at night by the stubborn pattern of male academic underachievement. Remember Blaisman et al.'s second scenario? Students intend to use effective strategies but, when they've left revision too late, they discard them like a needy and nagging partner. What if the research suggesting that it's boys who are far more likely to use rubbish revision techniques is just the tip of the Titanic iceberg? What if, in the other studies, boys are also (invisibly) accounting for the shoddiest study skills?

Are boys overconfident in their abilities?

There's another problem that can lead to boys sinking academically. Not only are boys more likely to use substandard study techniques, they also appear to be more likely to possess an additional belief that contributes to their tendency to study less frequently. There's a body of evidence that indicates that another reason why boys are less inclined to revise is due to their inaccurate perceptions about their own academic abilities. Research from 2006 by Alice Sullivan,[26] for example, suggested that boys are more likely than girls to overestimate their own potential. Like Sullivan's research, a 2013 study by Attwood et al. also found that on average boys predicted themselves a result that was one grade too high.[27] The boys in this study weren't utterly deluded about their likely exam performance: Attwood et al. found that 'just 17.2% of the over-predication were more than one grade'. And given what we know about the unreliability and inaccuracy of some exam marking – particularly in essay writing subjects like English literature and history – in certain cases the boys might have actually predicted the 'right result'. But there remains solid evidence that for many boys overconfidence in their ability might well lead to them doing less revision ahead of key assessment points in their life. I'm sure that experienced teachers will be able to picture many boys that they've taught who have overestimated their academic working standard and eased off on their pre-exam effort levels, only to find that they've not done as well as they might have. Now, for a boy who assumed he was going to get an A*, and ended up with an A, the impact might not be devastating. But I bet the same teachers can think of countless complacent boys who were certain they would achieve a vital pass boundary – like a scaled score of 100 in KS2 SATs, or a C grade in a GCSE – yet were left feeling crushed on results day after bagging a scaled score of 98 or a D grade instead.

Everything's going to be fine

Boys' it'll-all-be-alright-on-the-day attitudes aren't, however, just witnessed in subjects like English, where boys traditionally underperform compared to girls. The same brand of damaging contentment can be found in studies into boys' confidence about their future maths performance.

Research by Frank Pajares into students' confidence about their ability in mathematical problem-solving found that, unlike boys, girls had a tendency towards under-confidence.[28] Recent data from Craig Barton and Simon Woodhead's maths assessment programme Diagnostic Questions, found that while overestimation was the norm for both genders, boys were more susceptible to this phenomenon than girls at all ability levels. After scrutinising the results of over 7000 pupils, they reported that:

> all pupils overestimated their ability, with girls rating their confidence as 65.7 on average, compared with an average ability of 59.7 – a difference of six points. However, boys' average ability was 59.4 yet their average confidence was 70.7, a difference of 11.3 points.[29]

Looking at the overall research picture about gender, confidence and predictions, it's hard to escape the conclusion that, given what we know about the generally poor study habits and attitudes of boys, overconfidence is a dangerous trait that we need to help them recognise and avoid.

What can we do about it?

If we briefly recap the evidence about study skills and boys, we'll remember that:

a. study skills are vital

b. certain ones are far more effective than others

c. most students don't use effective study skills (or abandon them when they leave things too late)

d. boys are less likely than girls to use effective techniques, and therefore account for the majority of students who use ineffective techniques. When we control for study skills, gender attainment gaps disappear

e. boys tend to overestimate their academic progress and probably do less revision as a result

If we're going to harness the potent combination of effective study habits, attitudes and skills, we're going to need to do the following:

● **Make sure boys are using the most effective study techniques**

CASE STUDY 1

Mark Enser, Head of Geography and Research Lead at Heathfield Community College, East Sussex, narrowed the gender attainment gap in his subject by improving boys' study skills. This is what he did:

It's always difficult to attribute any outcome in our schools to one particular change, but when it comes to how we closed the gender gap in our Geography GCSE results I'm increasingly convinced it mainly came down to just one thing: the teaching of effective study skills.

We've made several major changes as a department over the last couple of years. These have, I believe, had a big impact on our boys' outcomes.

*The first thing we did was to **teach pupils what effective revision looks like**.*

We found that boys in particular responded very well to being shown the research into effective revision that stressed the importance of developing long-term memory and avoiding 'lazy' techniques like re-reading and highlighting notes.

Enser's approach recognises that, given the choice, boys are unlikely to opt for effective study strategies, like self-testing. They have to be persuaded that this revision will have a much greater impact on their outcomes than the 'lazy' and comfortable techniques that they tend to prefer. Research from 2009 by Karpicke et al. revealed that when students were given a forced choice between their usual way of studying and using self-testing 'only 18% of students chose to self-test'.[30] As Enser makes clear, boys need to be shown the advantages of effective study strategies and then be instructed to use them. At the end of the chapter, I'll show you a specific example of how this can be done.

What else did Enser do to teach boys effective study skills?

*In the Geography Department, our second key message was **don't allow opt-out.***

We stopped seeing revision as essentially an optional extra that we trusted pupils to do but never checked. It would be great to think that everyone would choose to revise throughout the course but we know that children are quite poor at delayed gratification, and the research suggests this is true even more for boys. We started to use homework time for spaced practice to ensure that they were regularly reviewing previously learnt material. This also meant they were always practising effective study skills and learning what worked.

We'll take a look shortly at some further examples of how you can increase boys' self-regulation and stop them opting out of home study.

The third strand of Enser's plan to tackle boys' poor study skills was, in my opinion, absolutely crucial:

*We were aware that for boys' outcomes to improve we had to **challenge false confidence.***

We needed to be sure that pupils really knew what they had and hadn't learnt. There can be a trend towards overconfidence that comes from simply having been in a lesson and then assuming you have learnt whatever was taught then. We started using regular quizzing so that they could identify gaps in their learning. We also changed the learning checklists we'd always used, so that they were made up of questions that needed to be answered before they could be checked off.

This was a really important move. One of the reasons that boys prefer to re-read revision material is that it gives them a sense of fluency through familiarity;[31] they've seen it before so they *must* know it. Using re-reading as a study tool therefore gives an illusion of understanding, fuelling boys' tendency to overestimate their knowledge. By contrast, retrieval practice offers boys no such hiding place. As Roediger et al.[32] explain 'testing permits students to have better calibration of their knowledge'. In other words, it forces them to face up to the reality of their knowledge gaps. It does them a service by denting their (over)confidence, which encourages them to compensate by working harder than they would have done using ineffective study techniques. Testing reduces boys' confidence but, counter intuitively, improves their performance! In the next section, where we take a look at self-regulation, we'll consider how you can prick the bubble of boys' overconfidence by getting them to face up to the weaknesses in their study schedule.

And the final thing that Enser and his team worked on? **Put study skills at the heart of the curriculum:**

> We made sure our curriculum also used principles of effective learning. We made sure that time for revision wasn't massed at the end of the course but was distributed throughout. We made sure that we reviewed previous topics at regular intervals and also found opportunities to explore where current topics linked to previous ones.

As Enser demonstrates, modelling and embedding effective study techniques in lessons helps students to make links to prior learning. And the benefits to male students don't just come in the form of revisiting previous topics. Roediger et al. assert that retrieval practice, for example, 'improves transfer of knowledge to new contexts'. So by placing effective study skills at the centre of the curriculum, you're encouraging boys to apply existing knowledge to different material.

Another huge benefit of making study skills an explicit part of the curriculum is that frequent low stakes testing will encourage boys to study more. In a classic 1971 study, Mawhinney et al. found that studying was most abundant and consistently spaced when teachers used a regime of daily testing.[33] By contrast, when tests were conducted at greater intervals, students largely studied just before the test. Like Heathfield's geography team, I know from my own experience that using quizzes at the start of each lesson, on topics to be learnt at home, greatly increases the chance of boys doing regular homework.

The Geography Department at Heathfield College clearly made great inroads into gender attainment gaps with Enser's four-point plan. I'm now going to give you some concrete examples of what this might look like in practice. Armed with this knowledge, you'll be able to improve the study skills of boys who are either reluctant or don't know how to study at home.

● **Teach them how to become better at self-regulation**

The EEF defines self-regulatory skills 'as the ability of children to manage their own behaviour and aspects of their learning'.[34] At the beginning of the chapter, we discussed the significant contribution that metacognitive skills make towards successful outcomes for students. To do well, boys need to have a good understanding of how best to manage their own study efforts. Yet, as we saw earlier in the chapter, boys are less likely to make use of self-regulatory strategies than girls, especially with tasks that are particularly complex or involving reading and writing.[35] When boys have poor study habits we tend to assume that they understand what an effective studying regime looks like, but are simply choosing not to follow such a regime out of idleness.

But the truth is that these boys lack a fundamental awareness of how to plan the study sessions, how to manage the time they have before key assessments, how to monitor their own progress and how to evaluate their potential academic success. As Matthews et al. make clear, self-regulation skills:

> ...are not innate traits, rather skills that need to be developed within students over time through the consistent and appropriate efforts of teachers and parents.[36]

Without explicit modelling, boys will not become better at self-regulation by chance. Rather than being an organic process, effective self-regulation is much more likely to occur when teachers – the expert learners – demystify the process for their students, the novice learners.

But what specifically can we do to guide boys towards the greater independence and understanding of themselves that is required of the most successful students?

○ Planning

Before they begin each study session, ask boys to go through a quick checklist of aims and methods. I recommend using something like this:

Question	Give details	Y/N
1. Have I got all the equipment I need for this session?	• Green flash cards • Calculator • Mathshelp login details • A4 lined paper • Art photos from my phone (ask mum to print these out)	✓
2. What prior knowledge do I have about these topics?	• Know about tree diagrams but struggled with product rules • Did a practice 8 mark question last week in class	✓
3. Where are my learning materials?	• Mathshelp videos 4b & 4c • Business studies exercise book and Ms T's revision guide (model example)	✓
4. What techniques will I be using today?	• Maths brain dump on tree diagrams • Put key points from Ms T's marketing model answer on flash cards for retrieval practice next week	✓
5. What will I achieve by the end of the session?	• Finish leaf drawing in charcoal • Be able to answer easier product rule questions • Know enough about marketing plans to be able to do own 8 mark answer next session	✓

A similar approach is necessary for study timetables. Asking a boy with poor self-regulation to draw up a study timetable is like asking a mermaid to roller skate. To begin with, it makes much more sense for us to provide them with a schedule or, even better, co-construct it with them, so they get an insight into the process. The timetable will be a reflection of the learning goals they have set, which as we know from Chapter 1 are vital in terms of increasing motivation. A decent timetable might look something like this:

			Week I			
Monday	**Tuesday**	**Wednesday**	**Thursday**	**Friday**	**Saturday**	**Sunday**
Business Studies Paper I 8 mark Qs	**English** Unseen poetry practice	**Biology** Improve 6 mark questions	**Physics** MDV (Qs with missing sides)	**History** Re-write sections of essay on gold miners in American West	**Chemistry** Exam Qs on copper and aluminium electric conduction	**Biology** Annotate section on evolution from class hand-out
Art Coursework Portfolio	**Chemistry** Bonding (See Mr H's feedback)	**Maths** Substitute numerical values into formulae	**Business Studies** Paper 2 Analyse case study and create flash cards	**Maths** Finding the nth term of quadratic sequences	**History** Bismarck and the trade unions	**English** Language P2 Q3 practice
Maths Probability & statistics	**History** Rise of Nazi party	**Art** coursework Portfolio	**English** Romeo & Juliet – marriage and religion	**English** Flash cards for A Christmas Carol key quotes		

○ Monitoring

To become effective self-regulators, boys will need to be shown how to keep track of their study progress. They will need to know what to do when they inevitably get stuck on a particular topic. They will need to know when and how to adapt their plans. One really helpful technique is a quick review of the previous week's timetable, using a confidence measure, like a score out of 10. Remember, though, to be specific about what this score means. I tell my pupils that 10 means *I'm confident I could walk into an exam right now and smash this topic*, whereas 1 means *I don't know a single thing about this topic*. Here is an example confidence monitor:

Week I						
Monday	**Tuesday**	**Wednesday**	**Thursday**	**Friday**	**Saturday**	**Sunday**
Business Studies Paper I 8 mark Qs	**English** Unseen poetry practice	**Biology** Improve 6 mark questions	**Physics** MDV (Qs with missing sides)	**History** Re-write sections of essay on gold miners in American West	**Chemistry** Exam Qs on copper and aluminium electric conduction	**Biology** Annotate section on evolution from class hand-out
6	3	4	2	7	I	6
Art Coursework Portfolio	**Chemistry** Bonding (See Mr H's feedback)	**Maths** Substitute numerical values into formulae	**Business Studies** Paper 2 Analyse case study and create flash cards	**Maths** Finding the nth term of quadratic sequences	**History** Bismarck and the trade unions	**English** Language P2 Q3 practice
8	3	6	5	2	3	I
Maths Probability and statistics	**History** Rise of Nazi party	**Art** Coursework Portfolio	**English** Romeo and Juliet – marriage and religion	**English** Flash cards for A *Christmas Carol* key quotes		
4	7	8	3	5		

When you ask boys to show you their confidence monitor, it's worth reminding them of a couple of things. First, at the beginning of their study schedule, you'd expect confidence scores to be relatively low. Second, I advise mine to make sure that a lot of the topics they begin with are the ones that scare them the most. Again, this will account for some low scores. Either way, it's important that they have an accurate summary of their weaknesses at this stage.

○ **Evaluating**

Finally, using the checklists and confidence monitor, get boys to reflect on the techniques they used and to think about how successful they have been. These reflections need to be turned into concrete actions, prioritising areas of greatest need. For example:

> ## Things to work on
>
> • Really don't get electrical conduction – speak to Mr S on Tuesday
> • Understand marriage in R&J but need better quotes and to work on my weak introduction
> • Must have been absent when we did quadratic sequences. Is there a video clip?
> • Go back to Cornell notes on Bismarck – can't remember much on this topic

In following your plan, monitor, evaluate cycle, boys will gradually become better at self-regulation. The process will become more intuitive. They will gain a more realistic brand of confidence. They will move closer to the Holy Grail of studying: independence.

● **Encourage them to study in a helpful environment**

As well as helping boys reflect on their study progress, we need to also ensure that they think carefully about where they study and what they do while studying.

Here are some key questions to ask boys about their study environment:

○ Can you see what you are doing?

This is not a rhetorical question of a metaphorical bent. One study found that, in addition to planning and organising more effectively, more girls than boys made sure that they studied 'in a brightly illuminated home environment'.[37] When I was studying for my A levels, I suffered unpleasant headaches after straining my eyes. This, my optician informed me, was a result of doing lots of reading under a measly 40 Watt bulb. It might seem like a trivial question but being able to properly see what you're studying is quite important.

○ Do you study alone or with friends?

Some people are great at motivating us to crack on with work. Others are easily distracted and can encourage us to cut short our revision sessions for a more appealing alternative. Personally, the idea of shared study sessions brings about feelings of morbid fear. But others are more productive in a communal learning environment. We need to find out which category boys fit into, and most importantly get them to honestly think about whether their study mates are raising them up or dragging them down.

○ Where do you put your phone when you're working?

To some boys, the thought of not having their phone with them at all times is horrifying. Suggesting they might want to forgo it for a couple of hours during study is like suggesting they could do without an eye or a leg. But suggest that we must. Because the presence of a smart phone is a huge distraction while trying to work through complex tasks.[38] The research suggests that having a phone in close proximity, *even when it is not being used*, has a negative impact on learning.[39] We have to be blunt when talking with phone-addicted boys about this. During study, it should be far from sight and looked at only during study breaks.

○ Do you listen to music while studying?

Boys will often tell you that blasting out a grime artist helps them concentrate when studying. But research by Currie and Perham[40] found that, in an exam, students who revised without music outperformed those who revised to music by over 60%. That statistic might just have them reaching for the stop button.

○ Is there any other distracting noise in or around the room?

According to Lucy Erickson, studies with adults show how noise disrupts our ability to think and reason clearly.[41] With children, however, there is evidence of an even greater negative effect on cognitive processes.[42] For this reason, Erickson argues that 'limiting background noise in children's environments should be a critical priority if the goal is to create optimal learning environments'.

Some boys, of course, will live in houses without room for a desk or space to lay out their study materials. They won't have the luxury of their own bedroom and will struggle to find a place of sanctuary where they can revise. In these circumstances welcoming, comfortable and suitably staffed study rooms become essential. I have visited schools that have made it their mission to provide an area in school where disadvantaged boys can regularly study before and after school. I have little doubt that this resource helped contribute to the increase in attainment for these cohorts.

● **Get them to recognise the psychological benefits of short, frequent study sessions**

As we've seen from the research presented earlier in the chapter, when it comes to studying at home, boys are more likely to procrastinate. And when boys procrastinate – a few more hours on the Xbox before completing sub-standard homework, or leaving their revision to the night before the exam – they inevitably impact on their academic progress. To teachers, this much is obvious. But what we probably don't realise is just how much the short-term avoidance of dull but necessary work can affect their mental health. And it's highly likely that boys aren't consciously aware of this either. A 2016 overview of research by Eckert et al.[43] makes it clear that procrastinating to avoid study 'reduces well-being,[44] increases negative feelings such as shame or guilt[45] [and] increases symptoms of serious mental health problems such as depression'.[46]

Frustrated teachers might well see boys who habitually dodge home learning as feckless and lazy. After all, they are the ones choosing to get their kicks on Snapchat rather than applying themselves to their list of irregular French verbs ahead of an important speaking exam. Yet the psychological research suggests things aren't quite as black and white as that. When boys select immediate gratification (short-term fun) over deferred gratification (potentially tedious study that will pay off in the long run), they don't actually get the fun part. In reality, as Eckert et al. put it, citing previous research[47] into the subject, the opposite occurs:

> Ironically, engaging in enjoyable activities while procrastinating do not increase positive but negative affect because individuals feel guilty about their task avoidance.

Like a dieter who feels disgust at himself after giving into temptation and chomping down a salted caramel doughnut, the teenage boy who spends his evening at the skate park, knowing that he should be revising for his GCSE Chemistry exam, has no real feelings of enjoyment. After the initial sugar rush of enjoyment comes the sickly disappointment and feelings of lasting guilt.

Tackling procrastination

Eckert et al.'s study indicated that, with training, procrastination levels can be reduced. By talking to boys with poor study habits, and acknowledging the negative and positive choices that many boys have to make each evening, we can begin to help them see that in opting out of study, they aren't just holding themselves back academically; they are also creating a dark cloud that hangs over their mood.

We know from Harris et al. that many boys are socialised to view study at home as an incursion into their relaxation time.[48] Yet we also know from the research into procrastination that deep down boys know this study is essential if they are going to do well in school and in life. Recently, I interviewed a group of underperforming, high prior attaining, disadvantaged boys at a school in the east of England. The school has done a magnificent job at boosting results. They've significantly improved the quality of teaching in lessons. But what became clear during our discussion was that some of these boys resented being constantly told by some of their teachers that they needed to spend less time playing football on an evening and more time studying. The teachers weren't wrong, of course. These boys were heading for disappointing grades because while they were prepared to work hard in lessons they were very reluctant to do anything much at home. They admitted that their free time was indeed occupied with playing football. The problem, I believe, lay in how the message was being delivered. Note the difference in tone between these two pep talks:

'You need to stop playing football every night and start working hard on your revision for GCSE Business'.	'I know you enjoy football more than revising the difference between sole traders and limited companies. But this knowledge is holding you back. Do an hour on it this evening, then you can enjoy a guilt-free kick about afterwards'.

● **Model every aspect of the study process**

Given what we know about the most effective study strategies, it's essential that as well as telling boys how much revision they should be doing, we break down exactly what the best study skills look like in practice. Has the business studies teacher shown the boy in question how to use retrieval practice for this topic? Here's what I would do instead:

This lesson, for those of you who are struggling to get started with your revision, I'm going to show you how to create some flash cards, which will help you massively, even if you just do 20 minutes each day when you get home from school:

Begin by writing a question on one side and put the answer on the other side

Here's my example:

	What are the differences between sole traders and limited companies?

	1.	limited companies - owned by shareholders
	2.	Shareholders have limited liability for the firm's debts
	3.	A sole trader is a business owned and controlled by one person e.g. carpenter or builder
	4.	They are easy to set up but owner faces unlimited liability for the firm's debts.

When you're doing retrieval practice, you must remember these things if you want to be an exam PASSER:

- *Pause before checking the answer. Don't just flip it over quickly*

- *Answer all the cards in your pile*

- *Save the cards that you find the trickiest. Put these at the back of your pile and have another go at answering them later*

- *Shuffle the pile regularly to challenge yourself with things you haven't studied for a while*

- *Explore your notes when you struggle. If, after two or three attempts, you still have no idea, look back at your class notes of the revision guide. If you're really stuck, ask me to go back over it in class*

- *Repeat, repeat, repeat. Don't bin the cards you answered easily first time. You'll still get a long-term memory boost from repeatedly testing yourself with them*

When we think of boys and homework, boys and revision, and boys and homework, it's easy to fall into fatalistic thinking. They're just not organised. They just lack the focus. They just aren't willing to revise. They'll never see the point of studying for tests. My experience of teaching boys successfully, and the research into effective study skills, very much suggests otherwise. In their summary of the main benefits of low stakes testing, Roediger et al.[49] looked at how students felt about a potentially dry routine of daily quizzes. But far from resenting the treadmill of memory tests, students reported feeling grateful for the chance to practise key questions and topics. They reported greater attendance and felt that they paid more attention. They felt that they had a better understanding of what they'd learned. Now think about the boys in your school. The ones who are falling behind in your class. The ones who are living examples of the grim statistics from the start of the chapter. Just imagine how well they could do if they knew a) how to study more effectively, b) got better outcomes and c) enjoyed themselves along the way. That really is something to get excited about.

How can I improve the study skills of the boys I teach?

STEPS TO SUCCESS

1 EFFECTIVE
Make sure boys use the most effective study techniques

2 MODEL
Model how to use these techniques

3 TEACH
Teach them about self-regulation

4 HELP
Help them study in the best environment

5 FOCUS
Focus on short, frequent study sessions

Notes

1 Crede, M., & Kuncel, N.R. (2008) 'Study habits, skills, and attitudes: the third pillar supporting collegiate academic performance', *Perspectives on Psychological Science*, 3:6, pp. 425–453.

2 Fisher, D., & Frey, N. (2017). Teaching Study Skills. *The Reading Teacher*, 71:3, pp. 373–378.

3 Dunlosky J., Rawson K.A., Marsh, E.J., Nathan, M.J., & Willingham D.T. (2013) 'Improving students' learning with effective learning techniques: promising directions from cognitive and educational psychology', *Psychological Science in the Public Interest*, 14:1, pp. 4–58.

4 Ibid.

5 Toppino, T.C., Kasserman, J.E., & Mracek, W.A. (1991) 'The effect of spacing repetitions on the recognition memory of young children and adults', *Journal of Experimental Child Psychology*, 51:1, pp. 123–138 and Toppino, T.C. (1991) 'The spacing effect in young children's free recall: Support for automatic-process explanations', *Memory & Cognition*, 19:2, pp. 159–167.

6 Karpicke, J.D., Blunt, J.R., & Smith, M.A. (2016) 'retrieval-based learning: positive effects of retrieval practice in elementary school children', *Frontiers in psychology*, 7, pp. 350.

7 Aslan, A., & Bäuml, K.-H.T. (2016) 'Testing enhances subsequent learning in older but not in younger elementary school children', *Developmental Science*, 19:6, pp. 992–998 and Lipowski, S.L., Pyc, M.A., Dunlosky, J., & Rawson, K.A. (2014) 'Establishing and explaining the testing effect in free recall for young children', *Developmental Psychology*, 50:4, pp. 994–1000.

8 Ibid.

9 Karpicke, J.D. (2016). 'A powerful way to improve learning and memory', *American Psychological Association*, June 2016. Available at https://www.apa.org/science/about/psa/2016/06/learning-memory (Accessed 1st April 2020).

10 Karpicke, J.D. (2009) 'Metacognitive control and strategy selection: deciding to practice retrieval during learning', *Journal of Experimental Psychology: General*, 138:4, pp. 469–486.

11 Susser, J.A., & McCabe, J. (2013) 'From the lab to the dorm room: metacognitive awareness and use of spaced study', *Instructional Science*, 41:2, pp. 345–363.

12 Blaisman, R.N., Dunlosky, J., & Rawson, K.A. (2017). The what, how much, and when of study strategies: comparing intended versus actual study behaviour, *Memory*, 25:6, pp. 784–792.

13 Morehead, K., Rhodes, M.G., & DeLozier, S. (2015) 'Instructor and student knowledge of study strategies', *Memory*, 24:2, pp. 1–15.

14 King, R.B. (2016) 'Gender differences in motivation, engagement and achievement are related to students' perceptions of peer—but not of parent or teacher—attitudes toward school', *Learning and Individual Differences*, 52, pp. 60–71.

15 Duckworth, A.L., & Seligman, M.E.P. (2006) 'Self-discipline gives girls the edge: gender in self-discipline, grades, and achievement test scores', *Journal of Educational Psychology*, 98:1, pp.198–208.

16 See, for example, Wagner, P., Schober, B., & Spiel, C. (2008) 'Time students spend working at home for school', *Learning and Instruction*, 18:4, pp. 309–320 and Xu, J. (2006) 'Gender and homework management reported by high school students', *Educational Psychology*, 26:1, pp. 73–91.

17 Lee, J., Grigg, W., & Donahue, P. (2007) 'The nation's report card: reading 2007 (NCES 2007–496)', Institute of Education Sciences, U.S. Department of Education, Washington, DC.

18 Marchand, G., & Skinner, E. (2007) 'Motivational dynamics of children's academic help-seeking and concealment', *Journal of Educational Psychology*, 99, pp. 65–82; Ryan, A.M., Patrick, H., & Shim, S.O. (2005) 'Differential profiles of students identified by their teacher as having avoidant, appropriate or dependent help-seeking tendencies in the classroom', *Journal of Educational Psychology*, 97, pp. 275–285; Ryan, A.M., Shim, S., Lampkins-uThando, S.A., Kiefer, S.M., & Thompson, G.N. (2009) 'Do gender differences in help avoidance vary by ethnicity? An examination of African American and European American students during early adolescence', *Developmental Psychology*, 45, pp. 1152–1163.

19 Ablard, K.E., & Lipschultz, R.E. (1998) 'Self-regulated learning in high-achieving students: relations to advanced reasoning, achievement goals, and gender', *Journal of Educational Psychology*, 90:1, pp. 94–101.

20 Xu, J. (2006) 'Gender and homework management reported by high school students', *Educational Psychology*, 26:1, pp. 73–91.

21 Younger, M., & Warrington, M. (1996) 'Differential achievement of girls and boys at GCSE: some observations from the perspective of one school', *British Journal of Sociology of Education*, 17, pp. 299–313.

22 For a detailed discussion of this phenomenon, see chapter 3 of Pinkett, M., & Roberts, M. (2019) *Boys Don't Try? Rethinking Masculinity in Schools*, Abingdon, Oxon: Routledge.

23 Harris, S., Nixon, J., & Rudduck, J. (1993) 'School work, homework and gender', *Gender and Education*, 5:1, pp. 3–15.

24 Gagnon, M., & Cormier, S. (2019) 'Retrieval practice and distributed practice: the case of French Canadian students', *Canadian Journal of School Psychology*, 34:2, pp. 83–97.

25 Griffin, R., MacKewn, A., Moser, M., and Van Vuren, K.W. (2012) 'Do Learning and Study Skills Affect Academic Performance?–An Empirical Investigation', *Contemporary Issues in Education Research*, 5:2, pp. 109–116.

26 Sullivan, A. (2006) 'Students as rational decision-makers: the question of beliefs and attitudes', *London Review of Education*, 4, pp. 271–290.

27 Attwood, G., Croll, P., Fuller, C., & Last, K. (2013) 'The accuracy of students' predictions of their GCSE grades', *Educational Studies*, 39:4, pp. 444–454.

28 Pajares, F. (1996) 'Self-efficacy beliefs and mathematical problem-solving of gifted students', *Contemporary Educational Psychology*, 21:4, pp. 325–344.

29 Lough, C. (2019) 'Boys overestimate their maths ability more than girls', *TES Online*, 7th September 2019. Available at: https://www.tes.com/news/boys-overestimate-their-maths-ability-more-girls (Accessed 10 September 2020).

30 Karpicke, J.D., Butler, A.C., & Roediger, H.L. (2009) 'Metacognitive strategies in student learning: do students practise retrieval when they study on their own?', *Memory*, 17:4, pp. 471–479.

31 Ibid.

32 Roediger, H.L., Putnam, A.L., & Smith, M.A. (2011) 'Ten benefits of testing and their applications to educational practice'. In J.P. Mestre & B.H. Ross (Eds.), *The psychology of learning and motivation Vol.55: The psychology of learning and motivation*, p. 1–36, Elsevier Academic Press.

33 Mawhinney, V.T., Bostow, D.E., Laws, D.R., Blumenfeld, G.J., & Hopkins, B.L. (1971) 'A comparison of students studying: Behaviour produced by daily, weekly, and three-week testing schedules', *Journal of Applied Behaviour Analysis*, 4:4, pp. 257–264.

34 Education Endowment Foundation. (2018) Metacognition and Self-Regulated Learning. Available at: https://educationendowmentfoundation.org.uk/public/files/Publications/Metacognition/EEF_Metacognition_and_self-regulated_learning.pdf, (Accessed 16th October 2020).

35 See, for example, Ablard, K.E., & Lipschultz, R.E. (1998) 'Self-regulated learning in high-achieving students: Relations to advanced reasoning, achievement goals, and gender', *Journal of Educational Psychology*, 90:1, pp. 94–101 and Bembenutty, H. (2009) 'Academic delay of gratification, self-regulation of learning, gender differences, and expectancy-value', *Personality and Individual Differences*, 46, pp. 347–352.

36 Matthews, J.S., Kizzie, K.T., Rowley, S.J., & Cortina, K. (2010) 'African Americans and boys: understanding the literacy gap, tracing academic trajectories, and evaluating the role of learning-related skills', *Journal of Educational Psychology*, 102:3, pp. 757–771.

37 Hong, E., & Milgram, R.M. (1999) 'Preferred and actual homework style: a cross-cultural examination', *Educational Research*, 41:3, pp. 251–265.

38 There's an irony in me writing this sentence: I've just had to put my phone in a different room because I was getting distracted by the pinging and flashing notifications of my mates discussing the football results on a Whatsapp group.

39 Mendoza, J.S., Pody, B.C., Lee, S., Kim, M., & McDonough, I.M. (2018) 'The effect of cellphones on attention and learning: The influences of time, distraction, and nomophobia', *Computers in Human Behaviour*, 86, 52–60.

40 Currie, H. & Perham, N. (2014) 'Does listening to preferred music improve reading comprehension performance?', *Applied Cognitive Psychology*, 28, pp. 279–284.

41 Erickson, L. (2017) 'Background noise and classroom design', *The Learning Scientists Blog*. Available at: https://www.learningscientists.org/blog/2017/9/13-1 (Accessed 23rd June 2020)

42 For example Leibold, L. J., Yarnell, B. A., & Buss, E. (2016) 'Masked speech perception thresholds in infants, children, and adults', *Ear and Hearing*, 37, pp. 345–353.

43 Eckert, M., Ebert, D.D, Lehr, D., Sieland, B., & Berking, M. (2016). Overcome procrastination: enhancing emotion regulation skills reduce procrastination. *Learning and Individual Differences*, 52, pp. 10–18.

44 Van Eerde, W. (2003). Procrastination at work and time management training, *The Journal of psychology*. 137. pp. 421–434.

45 Fee, R., & Tangney, J. (2012) 'Procrastination: a means of avoiding shame or guilt?', *Journal of Social Behaviour & Personality*, 5, pp. 167–184.

46 Strongman, K., & Burt, C. (2000) 'Taking breaks from work: an exploratory inquiry', *The Journal of Psychology*, 134, pp. 229–242.

47 Pychyl, T., Lee, J., Thibodeau, R., & Blunt, A. (2012). Five days of emotion: an experience sampling study of undergraduate student procrastination. *Journal of Social Behaviour & Personality*, 15. pp. 239–254.

48 Ibid.

49 Ibid.

How can I give boys effective feedback?

What's the issue?

During their time at primary and secondary school, the average student spends around 15,000 hours in the classroom.[1] That's nearly as long as the Siege of Leningrad. Or the time it takes Mars to orbit the Sun. Or the duration of Cook's voyage from Plymouth to Botany Bay. That's a *lot* of lessons. Yes, we allow them to play games and eat and go to the toilet and watch telly and speak to their friends and see their parents and even sleep in between. But it's still a long time to spend reading and writing, doing sums, learning stuff, and answering loads of questions.

Throughout this time, students are given information about how they are getting on. Given the amount of time they spend in classrooms, and the number of things we ask them to learn, this feedback will be very important in helping them improve as learners. It might well make the difference between them being contented and motivated students, keen to crack on, or dissatisfied and demotivated students, unsure what they should be doing and why they should even bother doing it. Get it right, and the boys you teach will flourish. Get it wrong, however, and the boys you teach will be confused, uninspired and may well feel resentful towards you. With substandard feedback, instead of progressing on a rewarding journey of knowledge accumulation, boys will start to lose direction and stall by the wayside.

Why is good feedback so important?

Effective feedback is a fundamental component of high-quality teaching. It can have a dramatic impact on pupil progress. It helps students to learn faster, more efficiently and with greater confidence. Ever since the launch of the first Sutton Trust Teaching and Learning Toolkit in 2011,[2] teachers have been told the headline-grabbing figure that effective feedback 'leads to an extra eight months of progress over a year'. Yet, despite the impressive findings, ensuring feedback is 'effective' isn't ever going to be easy. Indeed, the same report cautioned that 'providing effective feedback is challenging' and that if schools wanted to improve the standard of feedback being given to pupils, they would need to invest time in 'sustained professional development' for teachers.

What does effective feedback involve?

To make the biggest difference to student outcomes, feedback must meet certain criteria on the part of the teacher *and* the learner. According to Gamlem and Smith:

> Feedback leads to learning gains only when it includes guidance about how to improve, when students have opportunities to apply the feedback, understand how to use it and are willing to dedicate effort.[3]

If you're keen to help underperforming boys make rapid gains, feedback can be a powerful weapon in your teaching arsenal. But, to have a real impact, it must be deployed in a targeted manner. Effective feedback will be:

- **Diagnostic** – gives precise, high-quality information about learning, ensuring that students know what they need to do to move from current standard to desired standard

- **Timely** – offers support and advice during, or soon after, completion of activities to enable students to apply new knowledge and understanding while it's still fresh

- **Acted upon** – provides students with sufficient opportunities to apply the guidance and improve themselves as learners

- **Understandable** – recognises the specific needs of the student and communicates in a way that is clear, concise and comprehensible

- **Motivational** – encourages students to expend effort to develop their skills and knowledge, whether they have been successful or have failed to perform well at an activity

When written feedback goes badly wrong

Give boys feedback that meets these criteria and you'll give them a far greater chance of being successful in your subject. But much of the feedback that boys receive simply isn't up to scratch. Reading those attention-grabbing effect sizes about the impact of feedback, it's easy to succumb to the belief that traditional marking will automatically lead to better results for boys. The stark truth is that 'feedback does not uniformly improve performance'.[4] Indeed, one important overview of research into feedback interventions found that over a third of feedback given by teachers actually *decreases* performance.[5] Here are three examples of the kind of written feedback that, instead of allowing them to make speedy progress, could actually trip boys up:

- **Legibility** – A 2006 study by Weaver found that only 37% of students on one course categorised the feedback they received as 'written clearly' and 'easy to read'.[6] It may seem obvious but not being able to read a teacher's handwriting is far from ideal. Not wanting to appear too keen, many boys will avoid asking for clarification

- **Vague comments** – We teachers assume that our comments are clear and helpful; often they are confusing and woolly. Let's consider, for example, a frequently used annotation in humanities subjects: 'Too much description; not enough analysis'. One study showed how instead of encouraging improvement, this imprecise comment intensified student misunderstanding: nearly half of students interpreted it in a different way from how their tutors intended it[7]

- **Mistakes and errors** – When teachers fail to recognise the difference between mistakes and errors, feedback is less useful. Mistakes are careless slips (such as forgetting to use a capital letter on one occasion) that students inevitably make every now and then. Errors, by contrast, can be based on deeper misunderstandings. Marking an error as incorrect – such as confusing veins and arteries – without a prompt is counterproductive as students 'don't have the knowledge to work out what they [have] done wrong'.[8] Usually, re-teaching of this knowledge would be necessary

Written feedback that lacks thought and precision can hold boys back. And when we investigate the nature of the feedback that boys often receive, whether delivered in writing or verbally, we'll see how this feedback can decrease boys' performance.

Do boys and girls receive different types of feedback?

We know that effective feedback gives boys a clear assessment of their present understanding and actual performance, how we as a teacher want them to develop, and what they can do to reduce that gap.[9] Yet teachers often deliver feedback on students' work that is procedural rather than offering precise guidance on how to improve. How might we categorise the following feedback, for example?

- Criticising a student's scruffy handwriting

- Picking up on a student's sloppy presentation, such as using a pen to draw a graph

- Complaining about the state of a student's work area

- Telling students they need to fill each box on a worksheet

- Correcting every spelling, punctuation and grammar mistake on a student's work

Carolyn Morgan defines feedback that is focused on students' work habits – for example neatness or task completion – as 'managerial feedback'. This type of feedback can be both positive ('what beautiful handwriting you have!') or negative ('you've had 7 minutes to fill in that sheet and you've only done two boxes!'). The negative variety might appear to fit better into a discussion about behaviour management, rather than feedback. And, of course, students may well need to be tackled for shoddy presentation or careless spelling mistakes. Yet, when students ask teachers for feedback, or teachers provide an unsolicited evaluation of their work, and they receive managerial feedback comments, that is all they have to go on. Given this lack of clarity about how to improve as learners, boys will just focus on making their work fit into someone else's ideal presentation criteria. Research from several decades ago found that teachers tended to give more feedback of the managerial variety than feedback that focuses on students' academic performance.[10] And, crucially, as Carolyn Morgan's research has shown, at all ages, 'teachers tend to give boys and girls different kinds of managerial feedback'.[11]

Feedback for boys

So what do these gender differences in feedback look like during lessons? First, boys are more likely to receive managerial feedback than girls. Second, when girls do receive managerial feedback, it is generally positive, whereas boys tend to receive negative managerial feedback. Finally, boys usually receive this criticism and disapproval during activities; girls, by contrast, usually receive their praise at the end of a task.[12] Put yourself in this situation for a moment. Imagine you're a boy, plodding through a paragraph evaluating different attitudes to euthanasia. During the activity, you ask for some feedback about what you've written so far, to see if you should continue with this line of argument. The teacher, however, complains that you haven't copied down the date and begins to circle the words you've spelled incorrectly, like 'incurable' and 'lethal'. How would you feel?

Morgan's research revealed that boys in this position 'reported less interest in the activity, lower perceived competence, and less liking for the teacher'.[13] Frankly, I'm not surprised. In a fascinating twist, the researchers gave girls the type of negative managerial feedback that is usually served up for boys. Despite still receiving their regular portion of positive feedback at the end of the activity, girls felt exactly the same as the boys who received negative managerial feedback: uninterested, less self-confident, and unimpressed with their teacher.

A more recent study of 178 Portuguese students aged 13–19 also found a difference in students' perceptions about the quality of the feedback they received, with girls reporting a 'greater frequency of effective feedback when compared to boys'.[14] Negative feedback like 'write more' or 'you need to work harder in future' or 'you should have done better than this' fits what Black et al.'s research terms 'bland and unhelpful comments'.[15] Managerial feedback assumes that boys know how to improve but just aren't doing it. According to Gamlem and Smith's research, teachers who believe this are mistaken. One boy from the study offers a scathingly pithy summary of the frustration engendered by feedback of this ilk: 'If I knew more I would have written it – I don't know what more to write. Teachers should tell me what is missing'.[16]

The overall pattern of research, as well as my own anecdotal experiences, suggest to me that maximising the impact of the feedback we give to boys is a high priority for any classroom teacher. We need to think very carefully about not just *when* and *how* we deliver feedback, but also the *type* and *nature* of the feedback we give to boys, in order to do all we can to increase their achievement levels.

What can we do about it?

● **Cut down on marking and provide more timely feedback**

Lengthy written comments, usually eked out by an exhausted teacher in the evening, create an unacceptable workload burden. And, as the evidence shows, written marking frequently leaves the recipient feeling confused and has less impact on pupils than we might hope.

In the early days of my teaching career I noticed that the boys I taught paid limited attention to my post-task scrawl. This accentuated my frustration at the hours of additional labour. Nonetheless, I hoped slogging through books of an evening made a difference to the boys I taught. And did it? Research conducted by London South Teaching School Alliance suggests that the answer is a resounding 'no':

> There was no measurable difference in progress between the control and intervention groups in either writing or maths. In other words, teachers in the control group spent on average 6.2 hours per week on written marking, with *no additional impact on the progress of their pupils.*[17]

Is written feedback effective?

Let's just pause and reflect on these findings. Teachers work hard in the hope that the effort of written feedback will be reflected in improved outcomes for the pupils they teach. With boys who are lagging behind, this level of marking input will surely make a crucial difference? Not a bit of it. Teachers who spent around 6 hours a week writing comments did so for 'no additional impact'. Think of all those hours I wasted. Thank god I pretty much ditched written marking years ago.

Since I started using live marking,[18] however, I've found that boys are much more motivated by the precise and diagnostic feedback I give while the work is being done. My experience tallies with the Oxford University and EEF review into marking, which found evidence that timelier feedback – including verbal feedback – is more beneficial than marking done after the event as 'learners find it easier to improve if their mistakes are corrected quickly'.[19] I would argue that this is particularly true of boys. Especially the ones who require immediate scaffolding to prevent them drifting off when working through an activity. That tangible feeling of improving as a learner while working through a process becomes addictive. Success in the moment builds up stamina and self-confidence, and leads to longer-term motivation to excel in that subject.

Whole class feedback is another strategy that saves the teacher lots of time and, crucially, provides boys with 'high quality feedback which they can act upon immediately'.[20] Because whole class feedback frees up time from marking a pile of books, it allows the opportunity to focus on common misconceptions and plan follow-up activities for different groups within the class – such as preparing episodes of re-teaching or planning more nuanced modelled examples – so that the class as a whole can develop as learners, by working on areas of specific need.[21]

● Think carefully about your reaction to boys' responses to your questioning

In Chapter 9, we'll see evidence of how boys often become frustrated when teachers narrow down choice or deny them the opportunity to give voice to their own thoughts and interpretations during writing activities. There are several studies that suggest that boys have a similar response to feedback in the form of teachers' response to their initial answers.

Expert teachers ask lots of questions during lessons. Questions to identify knowledge gaps. Questions to ensure all students are paying attention. Questions to probe and deepen students' understanding. But as important as these questions are, as teachers we can sometimes overlook the importance of how we *react* to the responses students give to our questions.

For example, when might a teacher ask an open question that's not really an open question?

○ The (rhetorical) question is more of a directive than an actual question: 'Do you think my method of solving that problem is more efficient than yours?'

Here the teacher is asking the student to agree with them. The subtext is *my way is best*. It might well be. In that case, just say so!

○ The teacher has a particular answer in mind and keeps asking, while students try to guess it: 'Can anybody think of a good word to describe the character's behaviour?'

In these situations, the teacher will keep going until someone gets the idea in their head or, more usually, until they have to reveal 'the answer'. This used to be a big flaw in my questioning and I sometimes still have to apologise to my class when I catch myself doing it.

○ 'How would you evaluate X?'

This question goes wrong when a student gives an interesting but unexpected and potentially awkward response and the teacher shuts down that line of discussion. As Smith and Higgins illustrate, the subtext here is 'go where I want you to go, and think within the limits of what I want you to think'.[22]

We have ways of making you think

Now, there may well be good reasons why teachers close down these unanticipated lines of discussion. There may not be time to consider the 'unexpected' contribution. Or the student might be jumping ahead to a future learning episode and the class may miss out on a key part of the learning process if the teacher allows the current instruction to be derailed. If this is the case, however, teachers need to communicate this with the class. Boys are especially liable to feel frustrated – and might decide to withdraw from future discussions – if they feel that their thoughtful and astute contributions have been shut down. They will also become annoyed if they feel that the teacher has closed down an interesting avenue of exploration for reasons other than time and curriculum progression. Back in 1992, Alexander noted that pupil responses to questions by primary school teachers were either embraced or overlooked, not as a result of their quality but dependent on whether they fitted the teacher's planned expectations for the lesson.[23] Furthermore, Smith and Higgins contend that:

> unpredicted pupil responses, which lie outside of a teacher's comfort zone, may be particularly troublesome for teachers who lack comfort in their subject knowledge.

As Smith and Higgins explain, Newton and Newton's 2001 research provides further support for the view that teacher feedback to student responses can be shaped by subject knowledge deficits.[24] Newton and Newton found that where primary school teachers lacked a science background, they 'avoided using open questions and discouraged the formulation of pupils' own questions and speculations'.[25]

During the many lessons I've observed over the years, I've seen this happen so often, especially with vocal boys. One of them gives a well thought through but unorthodox response to a question. The teacher becomes flummoxed and their feedback either disregards the student's response or attempts to bluster on through, rather than saying 'that's a fascinating point. I'm going to think more about this and we'll return to it next time'. In my experience, boys quickly lose respect for teachers who deny them a voice when they ask legitimately awkward questions. All too soon, these boys become reluctant to play the game of answering questions purely on the teacher's terms.

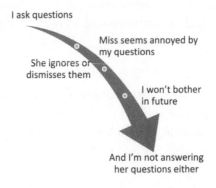

● Have high expectations to ensure boys act upon your feedback

Effective feedback can inspire boys to strive for improvement, even when their work has not met the required standard. Yet, whether it's verbal or written, for feedback to be embraced and actioned there needs to be a relationship of trust between educator and pupil. As Yeager et al. indicate in their fascinating 2014 study:

> Mistrust can lead people to view critical feedback as a sign of the evaluator's indifference, antipathy, or bias, leading them to dismiss rather than accept it.[26]

The 2007 research of Hattie and Timperley supports this viewpoint, contending that:

> The climate of the classroom is critical, particularly if disconfirmation and corrective feedback at any level is to be welcomed and used by the students.[27]

In Chapter 1, we learnt that, compared to girls, boys tend to take less pride in their own productivity in lessons.[28] Chapter 2 illustrated how across primary and secondary education, boys are more likely than girls to come into conflict in their relationships with teachers.[29]

So how can we convince boys to place trust in us, thereby motivating them to engage with critiques of their work? According to Yeager et al.'s innovative study, attaching 'a note communicating [the teacher's] high standards and belief in the recipient's ability to reach them' resulted in improved motivation and learning outcomes. They noticed that the effect of this note of encouragement had a particularly strong impact on students who felt 'more mistrusting of school'.[30] And what did the note say? It read simply: 'I'm giving you these comments because I have high expectations and I know you can reach them'. Now, I'm not advocating writing extra messages for boys who might be reluctant to act on feedback. The workload implications are too heavy for the average classroom teacher. But Yeager et al.'s research suggests to me that there could be possible advantages to private *verbal* conversations of this nature before crucial written feedback is administered.

● Avoid giving managerial feedback

Earlier in the chapter, we looked at Carolyn Morgan's research[31] into boys and negative managerial feedback. As the study goes back nearly twenty years, you might argue that it's dated and that our understanding of feedback has moved on considerably since then. Some seminal feedback studies have undoubtedly helped raise the profile, and to an extent the quality, of feedback. But from my experience of talking to teachers in lots of different schools, observing lessons and looking at students' books, I'd argue that boys are still more likely to get a raw deal when feedback is dealt out.

	Ben, you can do much better than this. You need to complete each section.
	Target: Capital letters for proper nouns

	Jemima, this is an excellent piece of writing.
	Target: Select evidence to support your points in the second paragraph. Use the adverb 'specifically' to make your points clear.

All too often, I see girls getting feedback that moves them on as learners and boys getting feedback that has less to do with learning and performance and more to do with whether they have complied with certain procedures that will often make little difference to their future progress. The 2016 review into written feedback by Oxford University and the EEF[32] argued that:

> There is some evidence to suggest that when teachers mark essays, a large majority of their comments focus on spelling, grammar and word choice, rather than content, organisation or the construction of arguments.

Red all over

I'm an English teacher. Give me a spare 15 minutes and I'll happily seize a red biro and scribble scarlet corrections all over some hapless student's work. Yet, I resist the urge to do this. Partly, I resist because the research tells me that highlighting mistakes can be helpful but that correcting the work is probably 'no more effective than not marking the work at all'.[33] But I also resist because I know that an obsession with SPaG[34] often means that students are getting feedback on only a small part of the success criteria. For subjects like GCSE History or GCSE Religious Studies, for example, SPaG might be worth just 5% of the marks. In this context, SPaG marks are not insignificant, of course, and are worth prioritising your feedback on from time to time. In KS2 English, given the demands of the SATs, SPaG mistakes will demand greater attention during feedback. Nonetheless, at secondary level I frequently see girls receiving formative, diagnostic feedback, such as 'now develop your answer by considering Islamic attitudes to the causes of crime'. Meanwhile, underperforming boys are often directed to respond to negative managerial feedback, such as 'use capital letters correctly' or 'you need to finish each question on the worksheet'. As a result of gendered approaches to feedback, attainment gaps can become attainment gulfs.

● **Move away from feedback involving task completion and performance goals**

When boys adopt performance goals, as we saw in Chapter 1, they are more focused on appearing competent and prefer feedback that makes them feel good, rather than wanting to genuinely improve their learning. They'll choose easier activities and, as we'll discuss in more detail in the next chapter, will avoid optional extension tasks. Research by Bronwen Cowie, using interviews conducted with secondary school pupils in New Zealand in 2005,[35] found that when pupils were given feedback focused on *learning or mastery goals* (i.e. acquiring new knowledge and skills and getting better at a subject over time), they viewed assessment for learning as the responsibility of both teacher and students. They enjoyed receiving suggestions that they could reflect on and then apply as part of their ongoing personal drive for improvement. By contrast, when feedback was provided in the form of *performance goals* (i.e. meeting a standard that allows them to receive some kind of external benefit, preferably while outperforming others) students:

> ...viewed assessment as the teacher's sole responsibility and saw no role for themselves in seeking help to extend their understanding. They preferred feedback on how to complete the task, and described teacher actions to elicit information about their thinking as unhelpful, because the action took time away from working on a task.[36]

Remember that boys are attracted to performance goals and tend to avoid setting mastery goals.[37] Remember also that performance goals are more closely linked to low achievement than mastery goals.[38] For this reason, *conveying a preoccupation with task completion is just about the worst thing you can do when giving feedback to boys.* If boys are to succeed, high productivity levels are very important. Negative feedback, like 'You need to finish this sheet!', however, is not just futile but plays to the performance goals mindset that believes completing tasks is the most important aspect of learning.

● **Be wary of attaching praise and rewards to feedback**

We know that boys often receive a demotivating and non-diagnostic brand of negative managerial feedback. Should we, therefore, go out of our way to boost boys' confidence and motivation by attaching praise and rewards to the feedback we give? You'll recall from Chapter 1 that unlike girls, who are more likely to be driven by intrinsic motivation, boys tend to be extrinsically motivated, seeing learning things as a means to an end, rather than worth pursuing for the inherent value of knowing or being able to do something.[39] You'll also remember that in following the influence of external factors, boys end up feeling that academic improvement is something that they can't control, resulting in a loss of faith in their academic potential. It is probably for this reason that, for some time now, research has found that feedback has the lowest effect sizes when it is only linked to rewards and praise.[40] This research highlights the folly of our instinctive desire to try to encourage boys by serving up feedback with a hefty dollop of praise, often mixed with a splodge of rewards. Giving a reward point, drawing a smiley face on boys' work, or handing out stickers like communion wafers at Mass will probably send them a very different message to the one you intend. As Gamlem and Smith point out:

> Research has found that feedback as extrinsic rewards often leads students to place more emphasis on incentives, which result in greater...completion, rather than enhanced engagement in learning.[41]

In suggesting you stop giving boys house points, stars on Gruffalo sticker charts and raffle tickets that offer the chance to win a box of chocolates, you may well think me a monstrous killjoy. But in associating praise and rewards with feedback, you are constantly reinforcing those damaging academic behaviours and personality traits that many boys demonstrate. Namely, in saying 'Well done. Great answer! I'm giving you a reward point', you're conditioning boys, who are already more likely to be extrinsically motivated, to see learning as something that leads to external benefits, rather than something that offers inherent usefulness and satisfaction. I very rarely praise when giving feedback. I find that teaching effectively in a way that allows boys to succeed is enough for boys. Praise becomes empty. Superfluous. Research by Skipper and Douglas from 2015 supports my anecdotal hunch, arguing that experiences of success are enough to 'help children develop and maintain a positive relationship with their teacher'.[42] Indeed, their research found that where teachers gave praise about a student's ability, such as 'You're really good at maths' and the student then went on to fail, this led to 'the most negative perceptions of the student-teacher relationship'. You can, therefore, shower boys with empty praise. But if things go wrong, it won't sustain their self-belief. And it's likely that they'll blame you for their substandard performance.

What did I do right?

Another major problem with teachers' preoccupation with praise when giving feedback is that without a summary of why the boy's work is impressive it becomes essentially meaningless. Telling a boy 'That's a brilliant idea' without explaining what makes it so good is deeply unhelpful and leaves them guessing how it met the success criteria. If we provide feedback that isn't transferable to future learning – what Dylan Wiliam calls 'improving the learner not the task'[43] – then students will be stumped the next time they encounter a similar question.

Finally, we know from other research that because of the powerful impact of peer pressure in the classroom boys prefer discreet praise, as opposed to public praise, given loudly by a well-meaning teacher.[44] Boys often find public praise embarrassing.[45] They would prefer not to be singled out in front of their mates. They worry that public praise and feedback might lead to 'negative social conse-quences including bullying, teasing and belittlement'.[46] Instead, when you want to make it clear that a male student has impressed you, try and have a quiet word in the corridor, or make a phone call home, which research suggests works much better.[47] Or, if you really can't resist the lure of praise when giving verbal feedback, try to make it diagnostic and depersonalised. For example:

Move away from	Use instead
'That's a lovely answer Dylan.'	'What makes that such an effective answer is the fact that it considers two conflicting arguments and comes to a clear conclusion.'
'Jameela, can you tell me why Jordan's answer is so wonderful?'	'Jameela, can you pick out a strength in that answer and suggest a way we can develop the ideas even further?'
'That's not quite right Rizwan. But well done for having a go.'	'Thanks for attempting that tricky question. But it's clear that some of us are still getting semibreves and semiquavers mixed up. We'll come back to this next lesson.'

- **Only attach grades to feedback when absolutely necessary**

As we've seen, attaching praise to feedback is deeply problematic. But it's not just praise that can cause boys to interpret feedback from a skewed perspective. As Wiliam and Black's classic 1998 research argues:

> Where the classroom culture focuses on rewards, 'gold stars', grades or place-in-the-class ranking, then pupils look for the ways to obtain the best marks rather than at the needs of their learning which these marks ought to reflect. One reported consequence is that where they have any choice, pupils avoid difficult tasks.[48]

Harks et al. concur, arguing that, when given to students, grades:

> …mainly inform students about their individual performance in relation to the performance of others and, thus, primarily are referenced socially, little elaborated and not related to single, specific tasks or processes.[49]

We've all spent ages marking a set of class books, diligently adding ideas to con-sider and suggestions for improvement, only for the entire class to pretty much skim our comments, ignore our questions and focus only on the score, level or grade we've added to our feedback. *What did you get? What about you?* becomes a cacophonous chorus around the classroom. There are always a few boys who have absolutely bombed, grinning inanely, trying to persuade their mates and, more importantly, themselves that getting a U grade or 7% on a test is actually *really funny.*

The competition problem

When feedback encourages comparison with our peers, it inevitably prompts lower performing pupils to opt out or self-sabotage. As Martin Covington has asserted, boys are especially vulnerable to withdrawing from work as a self-worth protection strategy.[50] If grades are attached, struggling boys largely ignore your feedback and lose motivation. Meanwhile, as Wiliam and Black's research also shows, giving grades to high-performing boys as part of their feedback leads to complacency.[51] It's a lose/lose situation.

To provide boys with the most effective feedback we need to ensure that the focus is on getting them to think hard and make continual improvement over time. We must eschew feedback that a) praises boys' bog standard efforts, b) focuses on their 'ability' (especially when it involves competing with others) or c) fixates on task completion. Giving the most effective feedback possible isn't easy. But if you're going to get boys excelling in your classroom, it's an absolute priority.

How can I give boys effective feedback?

STEPS TO SUCCESS

1 **INEFFECTIVE** Don't waste time on ineffective marking

2 **ENSURE** Ensure that feedback is acted upon

3 **AVOID** Avoid managerial feedback

4 **DITCH** Ditch the praise and grades

5 **DIAGNOSTIC** Give boys diagnostic feedback

Notes

1 Thorp, H.S., Burden, R.L., & Fraser, B.J. (1994) 'Assessing and improving classroom environment', *School Science Review,* 75, pp. 107–113.
2 An updated toolkit has since been produced: Education Endowment Foundation (2018), Sutton Trust-Education Endowment Foundation Teaching and Learning Toolkit (London: Education Endowment Foundation).
3 Gamlem, S.M., & Smith, K. (2013) 'Student perceptions of classroom feedback', *Assessment in Education: Principles, Policy & Practice,* 20:2, pp. 150–169.
4 Balcazar, F., Hopkins, B.L., & Suarez, Y. (1985) 'A critical, objective review of performance feedback', *Journal of Organizational Behavior Management,* 7, pp. 65–89.
5 Kluger, A.N., & DeNisi, A. (1996) 'The effects of feedback interventions on performance: a historical review, a meta-analysis, and a preliminary feedback intervention theory', *Psychological Bulletin,* 119: 2, pp. 254–284.

6 Weaver, M.R. (2006) 'Do students value feedback? Student perceptions of tutors' written responses', *Assessment & Evaluation in Higher Education*, 31:3, pp. 379–394.

7 Chanock, K. (2000) 'Comments on essays: do students understand what tutors write?', *Teaching in Higher Education*, 5:1, pp. 95–105.

8 Elliott, V., Baird, J., Hopfenbeck, T., Ingram, J., Richardson J., Coleman, R. Thompson, I., Usher, N., & Zantout, M. (2016) 'A marked improvement? A review of the evidence on written marking', Education Endowment Fund.

9 Hattie, J. (2009) *Visible Learning: A Synthesis of Over 800 Meta-analyses Relating to Achievement*, New York: Routledge.

10 See Blumenfeld, P., Hamilton, V., Bossert, S.T., Wessels, K., & Meece, J. (1983) 'Teacher talk and student thought: socialization into the student role', in Levine, J.M., & Wang, M.C. (Eds.) *Teacher and student perceptions: Implications for learning*, Hillsdale, NJ: Erlbaum; and Eccles, J.S., & Blumenfeld, P. (1985) 'Classroom experiences and student gender: are there differences and do they matter?', In Wilkinson, L.C., & Marrett, C.B. (Eds.) *Gender Influences in Classroom Interaction*, Orlando, FL: Academic Press.

11 Morgan, C. (2001) 'The effects of negative managerial feedback on student motivation: implications for gender differences in teacher–student relations', *Sex Roles*, 44, pp. 513–535.

12 See, for example, Eccles, J.S., & Blumenfeld, P. (1985) 'Classroom experiences and student gender: are there differences and do they matter?', In Wilkinson, L.C., & Marrett, C.B. (Eds.) *Gender Influences in Classroom Interaction*, Orlando, FL: Academic Press, and Baker, D. (1987) 'Sex differences in classroom interactions in secondary science', *The Journal of Classroom Interaction*, 22:2, pp. 6–12.

13 Ibid.

14 Carvalho, C., Santos, J., Conboy, J., & Martins, D. (2014) 'Teachers' feedback: exploring differences in students' perceptions', *Procedia - Social and Behavioural Sciences*, 159, pp. 169–173.

15 Black, P., Harrison, C., Lee, C., Marshall, B., and Wiliam, D. (2003) *Assessment for Learning: Putting it into Practice*, Maidenhead, U.K.: Open University Press.

16 Ibid.

17 London South Teaching School Alliance (2018) *Mark Less, Mark Better! A How-to Guide*, London South Teaching School Alliance. (my italics)

18 Live marking is written feedback that is given during the lesson – i.e. as students as working on a task. We will look at this technique in detail in the next chapter.

19 Ibid.

20 Ibid.

21 For excellent advice on how to implement whole class feedback in your classroom, see Lee, R. (2017) 'On valuable feedback that supports teacher wellbeing', thelearningprofession.com, 30th March 2017. Available at: https://thelearningprofession.com/2017/03/30/on-valuable-feedback-that-supports-teacher-wellbeing/ (Accessed 30th October 2020).

22 Smith, H., & Higgins, S. (2006) 'Opening classroom interaction: the importance of feedback', *Cambridge Journal of Education*, 36:4, pp. 485–502.

23 Alexander, R. (1992) *Policy and Practice in Primary Education*, p. 78, London, Routledge.

24 Newton, D., & Newton, L. (2001) 'Subject content knowledge and teacher talk in the primary science classroom', *European Journal of Teacher Education*, 24:3, pp. 369–379.

25 Ibid.

26 Yeager, D., Purdie-Vaughns, V., Garcia, J., Apfel, N., Brzustoski, P., Master, A., Hessert, W., Williams, M., & Cohen, G. (2014) 'Breaking the cycle of mistrust: wise interventions to provide critical feedback across the racial divide', *Journal of Experimental Psychology: General*, 143:2, pp. 804–824.

27 Hattie, J., & Timperley, H. (2007) 'The power of feedback', *Review of Educational Research*, 77:1, pp. 81–112.

28 Fischer, F., Schult, J., & Hell, B. (2013) 'Sex differences in secondary school success: why female students perform better', *European Journal of Psychology of Education*, 28:2, pp. 529–543.

29 See Bracken, B.A., & Craine, R.M. (1994) Children's and adolescents' interpersonal relations: do age, race, and gender define normalcy?, *Journal of Psychoeducational Assessment*, 12, pp. 14–32 and Ryan, R.M., Stiller, J.D., & Lynch, J.H. (1994) Representations of relationships to teachers, parents, and friends as predictors of academic motivation and self-esteem, *The Journal of Early Adolescence*, 14:2, pp. 226–249.

30 Ibid.

31 Ibid.

32 Ibid.

33 Ibid.

34 Teacher shorthand for 'spelling, punctuation and grammar'.

35 Cowie, B. (2005) 'Pupil commentary on assessment for learning', *The Curriculum Journal*, 16:2, pp. 137–151.

36 Gamlem, S.M., & Smith, K. (2013) 'Student perceptions of classroom feedback', *Assessment in Education: Principles, Policy & Practice*, 20:2, pp. 150–169, citing Cowie, B. (2005) 'Pupil commentary on assessment for learning', *The Curriculum Journal*, 16:2, pp. 137–151.

37 Ablard, K.E., & Lipschultz, R.E. (1998) Self-regulated learning in high-achieving students: Relations to advanced reasoning, achievement goals, and gender, *Journal of Educational Psychology*, 90:1, pp94–101.

38 For example, Schunk, D.H. (1996) Goal and self-evaluative influences during children's cognitive skill learning, *American Educational Research Journal*, 33:2, pp. 359–382

39 Vecchione, M., Alessandri, G., & Marsicano, G. (2014) 'Academic motivation predicts educational attainment: Does gender make a difference?', *Learning and Individual Differences*, 32, pp. 124–131.

40 See Hattie, J., & Timperley, H. (2007) 'The power of feedback', *Review of Educational Research*, 77:1, pp. 81–112 and Kluger, A.N., & DeNisi, A. (1996) 'The effects of feedback interventions on performance: a historical review, a meta-analysis, and a preliminary feedback intervention theory', *Psychological Bulletin*, 119: 2, pp. 254–284.

41 Ibid.

42 Skipper, Y., & Douglas, K. (2015) 'The influence of teacher feedback on children's perceptions of student–teacher relationships', *British Journal of Educational Psychology*, 85, pp. 276–288.

43 Cited in Hendrick, C., & McPherson, R. (2017) *What Does This Look Like In The Classroom: Bridging The Gap Between Research And Practice*, Woodbridge: John Catt.

44 Infantino, J., & Little, E. (2005) 'Students' perceptions of classroom behaviour problems and the effectiveness of different disciplinary methods', *Educational Psychology*, 25:5, pp. 491–508.

45 Houghton, S., Wheldall, K., Jukes, R., & Sharpe, A. (1990) 'The effects of limited private reprimands and increased private praise on classroom behaviour in four British secondary school classes', *British Journal of Educational Psychology*, 60:3, pp. 255–265.

46 Burnett, P. C. (2002) 'Teacher praise and feedback and students' perceptions of the classroom environment', *Educational Psychology*, 22:1, pp. 1–16.

47 Ibid.

48 Black, P., & Wiliam, D. (1998) *Inside the Black Box: Raising standards through classroom assessment*, School of Education, King's College, London, United Kingdom.

49 Harks, B., Rakoczy, K., Hattie, J., Besser, M., & Klieme, E. (2014) 'The effects of feedback on achievement, interest and self-evaluation: The role of feedback's perceived usefulness', *Educational Psychology*, 34:3, pp. 269–290.

50 Covington, M. V. (1998) *The Will to Learn: A Guide for Motivating Young People*. Cambridge University Press: Cambridge, U.K.

51 Ibid.

What do high levels of challenge for boys look like?

What's the issue?

Picture the scene. Reclining on an inflatable sun lounger, you begin an almost imperceptible drift across the hotel pool. It's late July. The sun is working gently on your light golden skin. You're coasting. An ice-cold beverage sits in your left hand but, such is the blissful inertia, you're reluctant to even raise your head for a refreshing sip. You're coasting. Sinking further into the cooling pool water, you continue your drift. Relaxation unknots your muscles and you unwind further. You're coasting, and it's the greatest feeling in the world.

Now imagine a second scene. This time you're not an exhausted teacher enjoying the essential respite of a summer break. Instead you're a male pupil. You might be 5, 10 or 15 years old. The age doesn't really matter. Hunched over a wooden table, your mind begins to drift across the classroom. It's late September. The teacher is helping a small group of your classmates. They are stuck on the maths problems you are very steadily working your way through. You're coasting. Distracting yourself by reading the number squares poster on the wall, your mind continues to drift away from the task at hand. Boredom permeates your soul. You're coasting, and it's a feeling of gnawing dissatisfaction.

Coast (*verb*)

1. Ride (usually downhill) on a bicycle, in a motor vehicle etc., without the use of power.

2. (*figurative*) Make progress without any exertion.[1]

In certain contexts, like the serene holiday scenario above, coasting is a delight. In an educational situation, however, coasting is the epitome of opportunities missed, of talent wasted, of potential untapped. In the classroom, coasting is the enemy of achievement.

How to let boys coast during lessons

It doesn't take much looking to find grim statistics about boys' relatively poor academic outcomes compared to girls. For decades now, we've tried all manner of things to boost boys' progress. Engagement strategies that are designed to motivate switched-off boys to learn, such as using competition, making learning relevant to boys' interests and creating opportunities for boys to be active during lessons. All of these strategies were designed with good intentions but each has been counter-productive,[2] leading to lower expectations of boys and, inevitably, all have maintained or exacerbated gender achievement gaps.

Other pedagogical solutions to the boy question have been equally disastrous. Instead of insisting that boys strive for the heights of academic excellence, such teaching methods have led to a dumbing-down of lessons and abysmal[3] levels of challenge. When teachers give boys unchallenging work, they are, unconsciously or otherwise, giving voice to a stereotypical view of boys as academically deficient, unable to rise to the same levels of success as girls. Only recently, a study from Finland[4] – a country much-lauded as a model for both outstanding teaching *and* gender equality – confirmed what earlier studies[5] elsewhere had outlined: teachers often perceive boys as lazy and behaviourally difficult, 'not…particularly bothered by low grades' and 'indifferent about achievement and school in general'.[6] Where teachers believe in this deficit model, they adjust their expectations accordingly, oversimplifying the curriculum. Where teachers believe that poor behaviour from boys is inevitable, they adjust their lesson resources in an attempt to entertain and distract.

Minimal progress, minimal exertion

Heather Fearn, Curriculum and Development Lead at Ofsted, once argued that 'it is impossible to meaningfully define "high challenge"'.[7] There's a lot of truth in that statement. Challenge is subject specific: what stretches pupils in maths and English are very different things. I do believe, however, that it's relatively easy to identify *low* challenge. For this reason, I'm going to start with what you *should not* do to challenge boys. Then, later on in the chapter, we'll look at some general principles that give us a far better chance of getting boys thinking harder.

The following are examples of pedagogical techniques and choices that, when adopted, give the *impression* that boys are making progress. When we scratch beneath the surface, however, we find that these approaches are robbing boys of the sky-high challenge they secretly crave. These approaches allow boys to make minimal progress 'without any real exertion'.[8] They allow boys to coast.

A. Busy work

The phrase 'busy work' can be used to describe lesson resources and activities which are designed to occupy students rather than promote the development of knowledge. Invariably, these tasks provide the illusion of hard work – a comfortable impression of 'busyness' – but when we peel away the veneer of effort, the activity offers little real educational value. Students look like they're working hard, but they certainly aren't thinking hard. And these resources and activities are disproportionally given to classes populated with underperforming boys. Researchers like Rubie-Davies et al., for example, have highlighted how boys who are not expected to perform well academically are more likely to be given 'few cognitively demanding tasks'.[9]

Thinking over task completion

Mary Myatt argues that when we design resources for use in lessons, we need to prioritise deep thinking over an obsession with task completion:

> ...too many tasks and worksheets focus on completion of the exercise, as opposed to making children think. This happens when the tasks involve activities such as completing the gaps, without having to think too hard. These are often ticked off, but when pupils are asked about what they have learned, or to recall information at a later date, they are not able to say... misconceptions can go unnoticed, pupils get a false sense of security and the teacher signs off work, often putting it on to a spread sheet, when in fact very little has been really learnt.[10]

What other kind of activities could we categorise as 'busy work'?

- Wordsearches and crosswords
- Basic cloze exercises
- Creating a simple poster
- Research tasks where students just end up copying and pasting from Wikipedia
- Painting by numbers maths tasks
- Copying from the board for no good reason
- Computer games that are only tenuously related to the learning
- Giving students jobs around the classroom that eat into learning time

Homework can also become bewitched by busyness. Activities like model building and making up songs will be relevant to some subject areas but in others have been thought up by a time-poor teacher trying to dream up a task for the sake of it. Look carefully at your own practice. Is any of what you give students designed primarily to conform to the set amount of home learning required by your school's homework policy?

The bad, the bad and the really ugly

Some lesson activities seem to fulfil a useful purpose, but probe further and you quickly see that they do little to enhance a student's understanding of the subject. For example, I once observed a geography lesson that featured a seemingly harmless anagram starter: how many words can you make out of the word 'sustainability'. While this task may have had a smidgen of value in terms of cross-curricular literacy, it did absolutely zilch to develop the students' understanding of sustainability as a key geographical concept.

Certain busy activities have zero merit and are simply indefensible. I recently came across a computer game that was designed for use in KS3 history lessons. The student – presumably a bored boy – gets to play the part of the rat, hopping from pillar to post, trying to make its way over a river, with the ultimate aim of spreading bubonic plague across the land. Let's put aside for a moment the question of the tastefulness of entertainment based on the death of millions. What historical knowledge is to be gained from this kind of busy work? I've encountered similar games being used in bottom set GCSE maths lessons. Once behaviour starts to slip the loudest boy is invited up to the teacher's PC for a spot of *Mathsblaster*,[11] a game in which you must answer very basic sums in order to annihilate hordes of invading alien spaceships. Other restless boys are invited to *watch* the mutant interlopers being blasted into nothingness.

Wordsearches also belong to the ranks of the unforgiven. The teacher pretends to themselves that students are picking up useful vocabulary during the completion of the grid. Yet, they know deep down that the students are thinking only about locating random collections of letters. Nothing is gained, save for a few minutes of tranquillity.

A harmless distraction?

Some might argue that this sort of thing is harmless: an innocuous distraction for boys who might otherwise lose all focus. I would argue, however, that there are two things wrong with this argument. First, in dumbing down our lesson materials in this way, we are advertising our lower expectations of boys. When we use them at the start of the lesson, we are seeking merely to pacify, rather than inspire. When we use them as 'breaks' later on in the lesson, we are effectively saying to boys that they are incapable of maintaining their attention for the duration of a lesson. These are the same boys who will be expected to sit in silence and complete lengthy SATs or GCSE exams. Second, in choosing to go down the busy route, we are sacrificing time that could be spent using materials that privilege deep thinking. Materials that expose boys to complex and fascinating ideas. Teachers – and, yes, that includes me – aren't slow to complain about there never being enough time for everything we'd like to cover in the curriculum. Well, in choosing to get boys colouring in the bubble writing of a poster instead of writing a paragraph on the difference between

Islamic and Christian teachings on the afterlife, you're *prioritising* busyness over academic progress.

B. Differentiated learning objectives and extension tasks

Each reader of this book is different. Some will come to it with an extensive knowledge of gender and social constructionism. Others might only be vaguely aware of theories of gender difference. Some will have worked in education for decades. Others might have just begun their teacher training. So, because of the range of pre-existing knowledge you bring to this book, I'm going to make an assumption about your ability to learn from it.

I think some of you are going to struggle to cope with the more complex discussions and arguments. I'm worried about whether you'll all be able to keep up. I know most of you will manage with the diagrams and the short anecdotes, but there are some meaty intellectual parts of this book that will leave some out of their depth. To be frank, I'm sure some of you won't be able to finish this book; you simply aren't clever enough. To make things easier, I've compiled below a list of three outcomes that a reader may reasonably achieve depending on their ability level. At the very least, I want every reader to complete the bronze task. Most readers should be ok with the silver task. But, let's be clear, few readers will have the ability to strike gold.

- BRONZE: try and read two full chapters of this book

- SILVER: read the whole book, using a pastel highlighter to pick out key bits of information

- GOLD: read the whole of this book then write a lengthy blog post explaining how you have already made significant amendments to your teaching practice as a result of its inspirational ideas

Some of you will aim for bronze because although you're very capable of writing a decent blog post, with a bibliography and everything, you just can't be bothered, or you're too embarrassed about the prospect of your mates knowing that you enjoy writing blogs about education books in your spare time. Others might take a crack at gold, but then realise that there's a big match on telly, so you'll ditch the blog part and settle for steady silver. Whatever happens, I'm not expecting big things from most of you.

Have I offended you?

The analogy of the previous paragraph was, of course, deliberately offensive. But hopefully the personal slights and lazy assumptions make clear my point. When we use 'Gold-Silver-Bronze', 'All-Most-Some' or 'Mild-Medium-Extra Hot' differentiated learning outcomes, we are saying that we expect much less from some students than others. We are advertising our low expectations to the class. And underperforming boys pick up on these ground floor-level, none-too-subtle preconceptions of their academic potential. The impact on motivation, effort levels and outcomes are catastrophic. Although these three-part differentiated outcomes are thankfully becoming rarer, they still live on grimly in many classrooms around the land. And even when they've been cast aside, they can still be found in other guises, namely 'extension' tasks. Extension tasks, also known as 'challenge' or 'stretch and challenge' tasks, involve providing an extra layer of challenge for students who complete the main task. For example:

Task: read two full chapters of this book

Extension task: write a detailed action plan of how you will implement five practical teaching tips from Chapters 1 and 2 in your own practice

The extension problem

What's wrong, you might ask, with this kind of extension task? In providing extra work for boys who happen to have finished the main task early, aren't we ensuring that they are adequately challenged?

Well, there are several problems with using extension tasks:

1. **Extension tasks advertise a teacher's belief that some children deserve harder work in lessons than others**. Now, of course, there will always be certain students who will pick things up more easily and will forge ahead with lesson activities. But in structuring the lesson using a main task/extension format, you are formalising these differences and ensuring that higher prior attainers will always surge ahead. This is especially true when main tasks privilege *completion*, while the extension tasks offer *opportunities for thinking hard*. Where teachers don't push boys they perceive as lower ability to tackle extension tasks, they automatically limit what boys can achieve in a lesson. And when boys recognise that teachers don't expect them to achieve, this leads to feelings of frustration and inadequacy.[12]

2. **Extension tasks provide boys with an opt-out**. It is my firm belief, based on over a decade of teaching boys, that all boys yearn for challenging content. Yet often they don't like to publicise this fact, for fear of derision from peers who might well see doing extra work voluntarily as deeply uncool.[13] Why ask for the harder stuff when you can coast by on the main task and then pretend you didn't have the time or ability to take on the extension? Extension tasks allow for a routine withdrawal from complex thought.

3. **Extension tasks discourage boys from following mastery goals**. Mastery goals prioritise a love of the subject and promote deep thinking befitting of a scientist, artist, linguist or any other academic. Performance goals, however, place an emphasis on meeting external criteria and finishing tasks. A performance goal mindset – which we know from Chapter 1 is much more common among

boys than girls – encourages boys to choose easier tasks and avoid extension activities that can make them feel or appear incompetent.

4. **Extension tasks can frustrate and confuse those that complete them**. As their name suggests, these tasks are meant to stretch pupils by adding in additional layers of difficulty. But in many cases their primary function is to keep the early finishers occupied while the rest of the class are still on the main task. This can lead to irksome 'more of the same' extension activities, which ask students to do a slightly different version of what they've already done. Where they are better designed, they still face practical barriers, as science teacher and curriculum lead Ruth Ashbee illustrates:

> [Some] topics do not lend themselves to many levels of difficulty. We might be able to get two or three levels of difficulty in questions on topics like the wave equation or uses of the electromagnetic spectrum, but after that there are no more levels of difficulty available without introducing new content. For these topics I'm not prepared to reserve the hardest questions for extension because they're not that hard and all pupils need to be able to do them. We can't just conjure up extension questions all the time because of the nature of scientific knowledge... Not all knowledge in science has the same potential for increasing difficulty of questions. When we put knowledge at the centre of our curriculum we can see that extension work actually cannot meaningfully exist in many cases.[14]

Under scrutiny, extension tasks can offer the worst of both worlds. In some cases, like the examples Ashbee gives, 'challenging' extension activities are not actually very challenging. In these instances, where extra layers of challenge can't be easily added on, but the extension 'structure' must be adhered to, tasks on the same topic are thought up for no good reason. In other cases, extension tasks ask students to move on to new topics, such as giving year 4 work to greater depth year 3 boys. These extension tasks, however, can leave boys struggling, as they haven't been taught the relevant knowledge to tackle new material.

5. **Extension tasks deepen attainment gaps**. Take two students: Student A is defined as 'low ability' and Student B is classified as 'high ability'. Each lesson, you give both students the same elementary work, but throw extra work the way of Student B when they finish the basic stuff. In today's history lesson, it looks like this:

> TASK: List three supernatural things that medieval doctors believed could cause illness

> EXTENSION: Explain how beliefs in the supernatural factors led to greater levels of disease during medieval times

The extension task is much more challenging. To answer the question, Student B will be drawing on, and applying, a wider level of knowledge. It will also require extended writing, instead of bullet points.

If this pattern is replicated over time, Student A will have little opportunity to access higher-level thinking. They will have fewer opportunities to build up writing stamina and develop their academic writing skills. This is what their respective progress will end up looking like:[15]

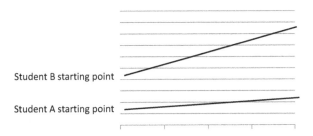

In implying that certain knowledge is important for some students but not for others, differentiated learning objectives are inequitable and exacerbate learning gaps. They may promote lower expectations of boys in a more subtle way, but extension tasks serve a similar function and ensure equally disastrous outcomes for those who don't access them. Through being denied the same opportunity to encounter harder thinking, Student A is allowed to coast.

C. Ineffective questioning

A consensus exists that effective questioning is a foundational strategy used by all good teachers. Just asking teachers to make sure they ask *more* questions, however, is not enough to raise challenge levels for boys. As Coe et al. maintain in their recent overview of the evidence about what makes great teaching:

> Questioning is already one of the commonest things teachers do, and the key to quality is not the number of questions but the type and how they are used... The key point is that just asking a lot of questions is not a marker of quality; it's about the types of questions, the time allowed for, and depth of, student thinking they provoke or elicit, and how teachers interact with the responses.[16]

When they are carefully planned and implemented, teacher questions ensure boys are challenged through exposure to deep-level thinking. Frequently, however, poorly thought-through and executed questions lower the challenge levels. Poor questioning lets coasting boys wriggle off the hook of challenge. Here are five flawed – but common – questioning techniques that do boys a disservice:

1. **Relying on hands-up questioning**. At first sight, seeing students putting their hands in to the air, in response to a teacher's question, is a positive sight. It suggests enthusiasm and a keenness to respond with an answer. In reality, the

most confident students do all the work, answering lots of questions correctly. Because of this, the teacher gets a misleading impression of the overall understanding of the class. Meanwhile, introverted or unconfident pupils take a back seat. This metaphorical back seat is, however, already crowded: squashed on this row are the able but underperforming boys – the coasters. For boys like this, the lethargy of opt-out is more comfortable than being routinely asked to respond to challenging questions.

2. **Allowing 'don't know' responses.** Letting boys evade questioning with a cursory 'I don't know' is another example of poor questioning leading to lower challenge. Is the negative response a sign of a knowledge gap, a fear of mockery for giving an incorrect answer, a reluctance to showcase their hidden genius, or a simple refusal engage with the question? Who knows? Certainly not the teacher, when they allow boys to opt-out with a cursory 'don't know'.

3. **Not giving adequate thinking time.** Perhaps the 'don't know' response is actually down to a lack of opportunity. A frequent failure to give boys adequate thinking time, to process and mull over the question, may understandably lead to them feeling rushed and flustered. Expecting a speedy response might seem like high challenge but instead it robs students of a chance to think. An automatic 'don't know' or a random answer blurted out is much more likely in these circumstances.

4. **Accepting basic answers.** In some lessons, simplistic and monosyllabic answers earn empty and unwarranted praise for boys. But allowing boys to dodge deep thinking by giving a rudimentary response – often in response to closed questions – is another sign of inadequate challenge. Conversely, trying to challenge students too early by hitting them with open questions, which require a complex response before they have the requisite knowledge, is a guaranteed way of confusing and frustrating boys.

5. **Inadequate checking for understanding.** Tom Sherrington writes persuasively about what happens when we don't check carefully whether all students know key information. A teacher, for example, asks a class to recall five things. Instead of finding out which pupils can list all five, the teacher allows individual students to reel off one thing each. As a result, 'teachers assume that students will hear the correct answers and self-edit accordingly. But that doesn't necessarily happen – especially for the weakest students'.[17] As we saw in Chapter 4, when we don't scrutinise the knowledge of boys by finding out *exactly* what they do and don't know, we facilitate their complacent tendencies.

In summary, three key areas contribute heavily to the levels of challenge encountered by the boys we teach. First, the critical curriculum choices we make. Second, our use of differentiation and whether we employ bolted-on extension tasks. Third, the quality of our questioning techniques. Get these wrong, and some boys will take it as a cue to metaphorically (and in some cases actually) recline, with disastrous consequences. We've seen what challenge gone bad looks like. So, what does the alternative look like? What should be our vision of sky-high challenge for boys?

What can we do about it?

When planning schemes, resources and questions, and considering how we structure our lessons, we need to have an overarching question in mind: *will this get students to think meaningfully?* To teach to the top effectively, we must:

● **Ban busy work**

It's obsolete. It's offensive. It's an insult to the potential of the boys in your class. It's an affront to your subject specialism and the years you spent learning how to teach. Knowledge is glorious. Being able to do stuff you couldn't do previously is glorious. There is no glory in a pass-the-time worksheet.

● **Abandon differentiated learning aims**

Crudely differentiated learning objectives based on 'ability' have no place in a high-challenge classroom. Instead, we need to stretch and challenge all our students, especially boys who are reluctant to push themselves. To get them to aim high, we need to give them access to the most fascinating things that we can teach.

A tale of two classrooms

In a unit of work on geographic models of development, a teacher sets a class the following differentiated learning objectives:

● ALL: generate a map about countries at different levels of development

● MOST: generate a map about countries at different levels of development and list three things that it shows

● SOME: generate a map about countries at different levels of development and write a detailed paragraph explaining what it shows

The PowerPoint that provides these lesson aims has the word 'all' coloured in red, 'most' in amber and 'some' in green. This colour symbolism helps to remind a section of the class that they are in danger of falling behind, which is true, because the differentiation effectively guarantees lower expectations of this group of students. While the teacher is satisfied by a group of students (mainly boys in my experience) managing to create a map, a minority of the class will do this *and* get on to the much harder thinking: using academic writing to analyse the data in front of them. Guess what's going to happen when the 'red' boys are asked to do extended writing in the assessment...

Another way

In a geography classroom in a school on the other side of town, a teacher sets a class this learning objective:

> Generate a map about countries at different levels of development and write a detailed paragraph explaining what it shows

This teacher has anticipated that a few students will struggle with elements of the writing activity. But, in the main, the teacher has avoiding making concrete assumptions about who this might be. Because sometimes students surprise teachers, by grasping things the teacher thought they might find too difficult. Given an opportunity that is denied to their peers in the school down the road, boys rise to the challenge and pick up on the expectation that they can cope with this level of difficulty.

At other times, of course, they do get stuck. When this becomes apparent, the teacher steps in. Depending on the number of pupils struggling and the nature of their struggles, the teacher might:

● Write a few sentence starters on the board

● Model a full or part-worked example under a visualiser

● Provide a step-by-step checklist of things to include to meet the success criteria

The language you use when deploying scaffolding is critical. Avoid saying things like 'Give me a shout if you're struggling' or 'hand up who needs some help'. Despite your good intentions, drawing attention to boys who might need extra support can cause embarrassment and resentment. So, try not to broadcast to the class that Toby and Seamus need some help. I find that phrasing it like this works much better:

> *If you're confident that you fully understand what you're doing, keep going. I'll be coming to give you some feedback shortly. If you're not certain about what you're doing, pause for a moment and look at the board. I'm going to give you an example to help make it clear exactly what you need to do. While I'm doing this, if it suddenly clicks, you can get back to your work. If not, keep watching me until it makes sense.*

This simple technique allows me to differentiate on three levels. But, crucially, they are all working towards the same outcome. Providing these sorts of scaffolds ensures that all students can access complex or abstract ideas. As Coe et al. put it:

> Scaffolding provides a gentler entry, but the destination remains the same. Lower-attainers may take longer and need more help, but the job of teachers is to 'disrupt the bell curve',[18] not just to preserve it.[19]

There is a danger, however, that too much scaffolding can lead to boys becoming reliant on the support you provide; if left in place when boys have already reached the desired level of competence, it can function as a comforting crutch. For this reason, you'll need to carefully remove the scaffold to ensure full independence. By now the supporting structure has done its job: rather than being the rarefied preserve of SOME, complex activities have been tackled by ALL.

● **Ditch extension tasks in most subjects**

My reasons for advocating the banishment of differentiated learning objectives also apply to extension tasks. They provide an optional element to learning, limit boys' exposure to powerful knowledge, send out dangerous signals about the teacher's expectations of a child's potential and, therefore, maintain or increase attainment gaps. When I discuss the consequences of extension tasks during whole school CPD, most departments recognise and accept the rationale for ditching them. But teachers of certain subjects are more reticent about disposing of their bolt-on challenge activities. They argue persuasively that their subject is different. That because of the way that knowledge acquisition works in their subject, extension tasks are essential. Let's now consider these special subjects for a moment.

But what about maths?

Maths is special. So is science. Other subjects, like computing and MFL, also function differently to many other subjects when it comes to knowledge structures.

In these subjects, it's often harder to teach to the top and then scaffold for support. As Ruth Ashbee notes:

> In some subjects, certain things simply must be mastered before other things can be... In mathematics, for example, it is really imperative to master things like the place value system and number bonds before most other things. In other subjects, such as history, you can learn about Victorian England without having first done Reformation England – there aren't as many, or as strict, threshold concepts.[20]

Because of the different nature of knowledge in maths, science and elsewhere, extension tasks are often used. For example, I see objectives like this used frequently in maths or physics lessons:

TASK: calculate density or mass when information is given in the SAME unit.

EXTENSION: calculate density or mass when information is given in a DIFFERENT unit.

This results in most of the class having a go at a worksheet, solving this type of problem:

A toy brick weighs 200g. The dimensions are 8cm by 5cm by 6cm. What is its density (to 3dp)?

A few of the class finish this worksheet. They are given the extension worksheet and move up a level of complexity, tackling problems like this:

An athletics medal in the shape of a cylinder has a radius of 38mm, and a thickness of 35mm. It has a density of 1.5 g/cm^3. Find the mass (to 1dp).

Some students finish this extension task sheet. Under pressure to maintain their productivity levels, the teacher scrambles through their resources for the next lesson and gives them another extension task. If they'd had the time to write it on the board, it would looked like this:

EXTENSION 2 – EXTEND HARDER: calculate missing lengths of 3D shapes, given the mass, density and some dimensions.

Impressively, these students grapple with a further problem:

A cone has a mass of 48g. Its density is 0.85 g/cm^3. Find the radius of the cone (to the nearest cm).

Because of the way that extension tasks have been used, during the lesson, the keen and confident pupils have completed extension questions and, as a result, have moved up a few layers of difficulty:

● Converting information to different units

● Managing calculations involving more complex shapes

● Solving problems where some dimensions have been omitted

The class have all 'done' density, mass and volume. But only a few have tackled the harder stuff. Meanwhile, reluctant boys have cruised serenely through the easier problems. When they get to the harder stuff next lesson, the pupils who moved on to extension tasks will already be ahead. If each lesson is an ascent of Everest, 'extended' pupils start at base camp, while the coasting boys are still clipping on their crampons. The gap widens and, come the harder questions on the assessment, the ill-prepared boys are left gasping for oxygen. Given the specialness of science and maths, what can be done to avoid this seemingly inevitable widening of knowledge gaps?

How can 'special subjects' replace extension tasks?

Recently, I spoke about boys and challenge to a school in Lancashire. The science department told me that moving away from extension activities had had the single biggest impact on boys' motivation and attainment in the subject. By teaching to the top and insisting that all boys attempted the trickier work, then scaffolding for those that found the work difficult, they had brought about a fundamental shift in underperforming boys' interest levels. Boys had also dramatically improved the content and depth of their work.

The science department had recognised that despite the different nature of knowledge in the subject, where students must grasp certain fundamental ideas before moving on, there was a way – other than extension tasks – to provide challenge for all boys.

But what does this look like? What specific actions should teachers of subjects like maths and science take when they wish to avoid introducing new levels of difficulty or introducing new content?

Mastery and retrieval over extension

Mastery teaching aims to ensure that all learners gain a deep understanding of a subject's threshold concepts before they move on to the next stage of their curriculum. Through a carefully sequenced and methodically executed series of learning episodes, the teacher gains a clear understanding of each pupil's progress through the key subject concepts. While this ensures a high level of challenge for all, and means that no struggling or indifferent boys are left behind, it inevitably leads to occasions where those who have mastered a particular concept require some additional work. But as Mark McCourt makes clear in his book *Teaching for Mastery*,[21] which focuses largely on the teaching of maths, it is imperative that this extra material does not involve new ideas or content. Instead, McCourt contends that this additional time gives students the ideal opportunity to revisit and consolidate previously learnt information.

Speaking as a science teacher, Ruth Ashbee concurs:

> Wouldn't it be much better for a pupil who has got all the questions right to spend "purple pen time", redoing questions from previous lessons for retrieval practice? This will often do more than anything else to improve the pupil's final grade. Having all the topics, questions and answers together in one book like this makes this practical in the classroom.[22]

Follow this approach and you can have everything. High aspirations for all. No students left feeling frustrated by a diet of mundane work. And no other students left twiddling their digits or surging blindly ahead into new territory. This is what high challenge for boys looks like.

● **Develop your questioning**

Earlier in the chapter, we saw what happens when questioning misfires. In order to improve challenge levels for underperforming boys, follow these basic questioning principles:

○ **Make sure everyone speaks in every lesson**. By rejecting volunteer-only questioning and embracing much more effective techniques like 'cold call'[23] and think-pair-share,[24] you will ensure that there is no hiding place for boys in your lesson. This will signal the need for them to pay constant attention, as it is inevitable that you will be asking them questions during each lesson.

○ **Give more thinking time**. According to an interesting piece of research by Robert Stahl,[25] after asking a question, on average, teachers wait for between just 0.7 and 1.4 seconds before expecting a response! That's about the length of time that it takes to open a can of fizzy pop. With no time to think through the answer, no wonder boys are reluctant to answer questions. So wait a while. The silence might feel odd but you'll get far fewer 'dunno' responses.

○ **Using probing questions**. Refuse to accept 'I don't know' as an answer. One effective way to respond is 'You might not *know*, but what do you *think*?' If boys are genuinely clueless, signal that you will come back to them later and ask them to repeat an answer that another student has already provided. That way there's no opt-out. But don't accept perfunctory answers either. Use follow-up questions to insist that boys elaborate on their basic first effort. Over time, they'll realise you aren't going to settle for mediocrity and will start to develop their own ideas without prompting.

○ **Check carefully for understanding**. Think carefully about what percentage of the class have understood something. Without raising the stakes by getting everyone to shout out marks out ten, think carefully how you will monitor success. For example, you might circulate and look at the books of certain boys as they complete retrieval activities, ask for a show of hands at the end, or ask them to chant out the answer at the same time. Whichever way you go, there should be no room for confusion or opting out where checking for understanding is involved.

● **Embrace live modelling**

As we will discover in the next chapter, boys find academic writing daunting. If we want boys to rise to the demands of the challenging work we're setting them, then we need to be showing them the process of responding and rising to challenge, rather than just the outcome. To do this well, live modelling is indispensable.

Barak Rosenshine's research concludes that:

> Students need cognitive support to help them learn to solve problems. The teacher modelling and thinking aloud while demonstrating how to solve a problem are examples of effective cognitive support.[26]

If you shift from teaching to the middle to teaching to the top, you'll find that previously recalcitrant boys quickly learn to love the higher challenge you provide.

But they still need that 'effective cognitive support'. Live modelling provides this by harnessing the powerful impact of **metacognition**, talking through the process as you create a worked example. This might sound obvious, but we often deny pupils free admission into the mind of an expert. That's you, by the way. Watching us cope with a multitude of important decisions – diction, positioning of syntax, evidence selection, argument structure – gives boys instant insight into a previously arcane process.

Seeing you go back and edit or correct work while you discuss your amendments is invaluable for students. It's tempting to view boys who are slow to edit as lazy; yet, in reality, until you show them what the editing process looks like, they actually just don't know how to improve.

Let's look at an example for GCSE PE:

> With reference to a named sporting activity, outline what plyometric and Fartlek training are, and justify why they are both relevant to performers in that activity. (9 marks)

The teacher starts to write:

> When you are cricket training you can use plyometric training. This is when you do stuff like jump up on a box to improve the power in your legs -

Then the teacher stops and says:

> *No, wait. That's not great. The explanation of the activity needs more technical vocabulary. And the opening sentence sounds very clumsy. Let's amend like this.*
>
> ~~When you are cricket training you can use plyometric training~~. Cricket offers an ideal opportunity to use plyometric training. ~~This is when you do stuff like jump up on a box to improve the power in your legs~~ Plyometric training incorporates jumping and bouncing into a fitness regime, bringing explosive power to muscles...
>
> *That first sentence is miles better now. And see how much better 'fitness regime' sounds compared to 'do stuff'? And using more precise anatomical words like 'muscle' instead of 'legs'? Now it needs an example of why it's a useful training for performers...*
>
> ...this means you'll be good at jumping up to catch a ball.
>
> *Hmm, that's not very good, is it year 10? So, I want you all to think for 30 seconds of a more specific example of why a cricketer might need explosive power to jump. Okay, Pete, start us off – what should we use instead?*

Eventually, the teacher reaches this stage:

> ~~...this means you'll be good at jumping up to catch a ball.~~ This would be ~~very helpful~~ beneficial for fielding in the slips, for example, which involves long

periods of standing sedentary, then using the ~~leg~~ calf and thigh muscles to make a sudden powerful leap from a standing start to take a catch.

Right, now let's move onto the Fartlek part of the answer...

And so on.

Live modelling shows boys that success isn't something that comes as the result of a click on a PowerPoint slide. Success is a process of thinking, editing and reflecting again. Importantly, what it also shows is that *mistakes are okay*. And in a classroom where mistakes are okay, initially insurmountable challenges become doable, because failure is okay too. In fact, failure in the face of high challenge is an essential part of getting better at writing. Or anything else for that matter.

What do high levels of challenge for boys look like?

STEPS TO SUCCESS

1 **BAN** Ban busy work

2 **ABANDON** Abandon differentiated learning aims

3 **TOP** Teach to the top – no extension tasks

4 **REFINE** Refine your questioning skills

5 **STRETCH** Live model to stretch boys

Notes

1 Brown, L. (eds.) (1993) *The New Shorter Oxford English Dictionary*, Oxford: Oxford University Press, p. 429.
2 For a detailed explanation of the flawed nature of these approaches to engagement see Chapter 1 of Pinkett, M., & Roberts, M. (2019) *Boys Don't Try? Rethinking Masculinity in Schools*, Abingdon, Oxon: Routledge.
3 The etymology of this adjective is instructive here, I think. Describing the abyss – a dungeon of torment and suffering in Greek mythology – it is derived from the word 'bottomless'.
4 Perander, K., Londen, M., & Holm, G. (2020) 'Anxious girls and laid-back boys: teachers' and study counsellors' gendered perceptions of students', *Cambridge Journal of Education*, 50:2, pp. 185–199.
5 See, for example, Myhill, D., & Jones, S. (2004) ''Troublesome boys' and 'compliant girls': gender identity and perceptions of achievement and underachievement', *British Journal of Sociology of Education*, 25: 5, pp. 547–561 and Jackson, C. (2010) ''I've been sort of laddish with them...one of the gang': teachers' perceptions of 'laddish' boys and how to deal with them', *Gender and Education*, 22:5, pp. 505–519.
6 Ibid.
7 Fearn, H. (2017) 'What does high challenge teaching look like?', *Schools Week*, 27th March 2017. Available at: https://schoolsweek.co.uk/what-does-high-challenge-teaching-look-like/ (Accessed 15th October 2020).
8 Ibid.
9 Rubie-Davies, C., Hattie, J., & Hamilton, R. (2006) Expecting the best for students: teacher expectations and academic outcomes, *British Journal of Educational Psychology*, 76, pp 431.

10 Myatt, M. (2020) 'Are our resources useful and beautiful?', marymyatt.com. Available at https://www.marymyatt.com/blog/are-our-resources-useful-and-beautiful, (Accessed 10th October 2020).

11 I might have made the name of this game up. But even if I could remember what the game was called, I wouldn't tell you, for fear that you might be tempted to use it with 8RIP during Friday period 5 lessons...

12 For example, Travers, M-C. (2017) *White Working-Class Boys: Teachers matter*, Stoke-on-Trent: Trentham Books.

13 For an in-depth explanation of how peer pressure influences boys' learning attitudes, see Chapter 3 of Pinkett, M., & Roberts, M. (2019) *Boys Don't Try? Rethinking Masculinity in Schools*, Abingdon, Oxon: Routledge.

14 Ashbee, R. (2017) 'Why extension work in science is often a bad idea', rosalind-walker.wordpress.com, 7th July 2017. Available at: https://rosalindwalker.wordpress.com/2017/07/07/why-extension-work-in-science-is-often-a-bad-idea-part-3-of-my-researched-rugby-talk/ (Accessed 10th October 2020).

15 I appreciate that progress isn't neat and linear, but my point still stands.

16 Coe, R., Rauch, C.J., Kime, S., & Singleton, D. (2020) Great Teaching Toolkit: Evidence Review, June 2020, Cambridge Assessment International Education: Evidence Based Education.

17 Sherrington, T. (2019) 'The #1 problem/weakness in teaching and how to address it', teacherhead.com, 4th October 2019. Available at: https://teacherhead.com/2019/10/04/the-1-problem-weakness-in-teaching-and-how-to-address-it/ (Accessed 14th October 2020).

18 Wiliam, D. (2018) *Creating the schools our children need: why what we're doing now won't help much (and what we can do instead)*, Learning Sciences International.

19 Ibid.

20 Ashbee, R. (2020) 'Vertical, horizontal, hierarchical, cumulative, integrative, discursive', rosalindwalker.wordpress.com. Available at: /https://rosalindwalker.wordpress.com/2020/02/11/vertical-horizontal-hierarchical-cumulative-integrative-discursive/ (Accessed 16th October 2020).

21 McCourt, M. (2019) *Teaching for Mastery*, John Catt: Woodbridge, UK.

22 Ibid.

23 Where students are asked questions whether they have their hands raised or not. Taken from from Lemov, D. (2015) *Teach Like a Champion 2.0: 62 Techniques that Put Students on the Path to College*, San Francisco: Jossey-Bass.

24 Students are given thinking time, before discussing ideas with another student. Finally they are asked to share their response with the class.

25 Stahl, R. (1994). 'Using "Think-Time" and "Wait-Time" Skilfully in the Classroom', ERIC Clearinghouse for Social Studies/Social Science Education.

26 Rosenshine, B. (2012) 'Principles of instruction: research-based strategies that all teachers should know', *The American Educator*, 36:12.

PART C
Developing boys' literacy

7 How can I improve boys' academic writing?

What's the issue?

It's blinding you. A threatening space, rectangular and blank. A whiteness that seems to take up an area of acres, not inches. Whiter than a winter snowstorm in the bleakest tundra. Apart from the faintest of parallel blue lines, repeatedly crossing the barren horizon, all is white. It's waiting for you to occupy it. To colonise its emptiness with your decisive and purposeful movements. But nothing comes; blankness reigns.

The blank page is an intimidating space for anybody. Even writers of maturity and deep expertise can be cowed by the prospect of putting pen to notebook, or making virgin incursions to the glaring whiteness of a Word document. But for novice writers – especially boys who lack confidence in their ability to express themselves through the written word – the blank page can be a truly cold and inhospitable place.

What is writing?

I'm aware that the question I've just posed is an odd one. Everyone knows what writing is. From the clumsy-fingers of the inquisitive toddler to the skilful calligraphy of the aged scholar, everybody understands the action and purpose of writing. Don't they?

According to Graham et al., writing can be defined as:

a goal-directed and self-sustained cognitive activity requiring the skilful management of (a) the writing environment; (b) the constraints imposed by the writing topic; (c) the intentions of the writer(s); and (d) the processes, knowledge, and skills involved in composing.[1]

That's a complicated definition. So, let's try and break it down by using the opening paragraphs of this chapter as an example:

a. The writing environment

As I write, highly uncivilised children are running around downstairs, sounding like they're trying to kill each other. But up here in the sanctuary of my study,[2] apart from the odd piercing scream of one of my kids, I'm insulated from the distractions of the outside world. Crucially, my phone is ensconced in a different room, away from my wandering hands and wandering mind. Writing is a complex activity. Attempting to do it in a chaotic environment increases the difficulty level hugely.

b. The constraints imposed by the writing topic

This is an information text. So, I'm aware that the purpose of my opening is to begin to explain to you the challenges faced by reluctant writers, especially boys. I'm also very much aware that my reader is a teacher, or someone with an interest in education, or perhaps a parent who is keen to support their son with his learning. At the same time, I want the text to be entertaining and stylistically appealing, given that I'm guiding you through academic research that is often as dry as the Atacama Desert. For this reason, I use metaphorical language to improve readability.

c. The intentions of the writer

But there's something else going on in my opening paragraph, isn't there? I'm trying to deliberately disorientate you as a reader. To convey my point about the daunting nature of a blank piece of A4 to an apprehensive writer, I've not actually used the word 'paper'. In doing this, I'm provoking a similar kind of displacement as the reluctant boy feels when starting to write. This is meant to be short-lived; I make it clear what I'm writing about at the start of the second paragraph, as I didn't want to outstay my welcome: you've picked up a non-fiction book about boys, not bloody French postmodernist theory.

d. The processes, knowledge and skills involved in composing

My literary knowledge allows me to play around with my reader. Describing an everyday object in a fresh but confusing way is a fancy device called defamiliarisation.[3] But in composing my opening sentences, I also had to make more mundane but nonetheless vital decisions. Where to put commas and full stops. How to spell 'parallel'. The order of the words and the sentence structures. All this flows through my head as I simultaneously tap away at the keyboard, ensuring the often conflicting and messy ideas appear before me on the white screen.

Writing is difficult

As you can see, even for an expert, writing involves a plethora of competing thoughts, actions and attitudes. Despite its complexity, I love writing. But sometimes I hate it. Sometimes I bash away at the keyboard for hours and all that emerges is dross. Imagine, therefore, a novice student writer. He doesn't love writing. He feels like I do on my bad writing days *all the time*. He doesn't want to sit in a quiet room and write. He doesn't understand the purpose of writing. He doesn't have my experience to fall back on. For him, writing is a mysterious and often torturous activity. A torturous activity that's a daily fixture during his time at school.

As Graham et al. note:

> Kellogg's (1987, 1993) research examining the mental effort involved in writing (at least for college students) showed that it approaches the level of effort expended by expert chess players involved in move selections.[4]

For the novice writer, working through these kinds of writing 'move selections' can be overwhelming. To stretch the chess analogy further, imagine trying to make your move if you physically struggled to hold the pieces, couldn't tell the difference between a king and a castle, and couldn't remember how a knight moves.

The importance of academic writing

Think of all the subjects a child writes about during their time at school: from early year's literacy, to primary geography, to GCSE PE, to A level biology. Each discipline with its own specific function, style and assessment criteria. During that time, the child will use writing to plan, recall, analyse, summarise, synthesise, explain, inform, influence, argue and develop knowledge. They will write very brief notes, and they will write long extended reports and essays. Writing in schools is a ubiquitous activity. Put simply, students who become proficient at academic writing will usually do much better than ones that don't.

Why do boys struggle with academic writing?

When it comes to writing, girls generally outperform boys. The evidence tells us that:

- Girls are more likely to be proficient writers who work at an advanced level[5]

- Girls are significantly more adept at remembering and writing the letters that form words on a page[6]

- Girls significantly outperform boys in being able to both express their ideas in words and the syntax of sentences on the page[7]

- Girls are more likely to embrace and manage complex writing processes, like planning and editing, than boys[8]

Why do boys lag behind when it comes to writing? Might it be that there is something happening at a genetic level, which means that girls are just more naturally gifted? According to De Smedt et al., this is not the case:

> Bourke and Adams (2012)[9] showed that boys and girls have the same cognitive resources (i.e. working memory functioning) available to support writing development and that boys and girls have the same potential for composing...[10]

So if there aren't any cognitive reasons, what else is going on? Let's return to the fear-inducing blank page. Might it be that, beyond the physical challenges of handwriting, boys' attitudes towards academic writing is the factor really holding them back?

Why don't boys like writing?

In terms of attitudes to gender and feelings about writing, the research picture is also bleak:

- Writing is seen by most students, particularly younger ones, as a 'feminine' activity[11]
- Girls have a more positive mindset towards writing[12]
- Different attitudes towards writing between girls and boys may emerge 'even at very early ages'[13]
- Generally, girls are more motivated to write compared to boys[14]
- Specifically, girls are far more likely to be motivated to write because they see writing as an activity that is worthwhile or enjoyable in itself[15]

Faced with this kind of grim evidence about writing beliefs, it's easy to perceive boys' apparent aversion to writing as a symptom of a wider apathy towards learning. But as Caroline Daly noted, back in 2002, teachers need to:

> develop a better understanding of boys' resistance to writing. Teachers frequently equate boys' unenthusiastic responses to extended writing... with 'laziness' or inherent male antipathy...especially in relation to girls, and can consequently develop low expectations.[16]

Writing is hard, but it's also fundamental to academic success. And for many boys it has the same appeal as the salad counter in the school canteen. For more boys to succeed, we must address this massive issue. We must get boys to engage with the idea and process of writing academically.

What can we do about it?

● **Train teachers how to teach writing**

Research conducted in 2009 by Kiuhara et al. found that one in two teachers had received little or no guidance on how to teach writing.[17] Given the critical importance of writing, how could it be that half of teachers felt unprepared to teach it? The problem, I would argue, is based on a dangerous assumption that is frequently made about teachers and teaching. We assume that because teachers have written lots of assignments in order to get a degree, and are therefore decent writers, they must know how to teach writing. But being good at something doesn't automatically mean that you'll be good at teaching it. Think of all the prodigiously talented sportspeople who have gone on to make awful coaches.

One example of the flaws in the assumption that teachers know how to teach writing can be seen when teachers hold a discussion in class and then expect that because the discussion has taken place good writing will follow. Oracy can indeed be a very helpful first step towards formulating effective writing. But Anna Beattie's 2007 research, which drew on her own teaching experiences, illustrates what happens when we assume that productive class talk leads organically to productive writing:

> I had been mistaken in my belief that a 'good' discussion would automatically lead to 'good' writing, and I believe the boys treated the exercise as a ruthless move (on my part) between an activity that was supported and guided… to one in which they had no foundations and felt neglected.[18]

Anyone for writing tennis?

Expecting boys to 'capture' the learning of a discussion without offering a model or structure of what effective writing looks like is like showing Serena Williams' serve to a young tennis player and expecting them to replicate it without any prompts. Not only will they end up flailing wildly, they'll end up feeling demotivated and resentful.

But it's too late for me…

In an ideal teaching world, ITT providers would place a much greater emphasis on the mechanics of teaching writing. As a PGCE student, learning how to teach boys to write an effective introduction would have been much more use than yet another seminar on De Bono's amazing technicoloured dream thinking hats.

For all you teachers already working in schools, however, it might seem like that boat has already left port. Don't fear. By dedicating plenty of CPD time to teaching writing, you will still be able to make a huge difference to boys' outcomes in your class. Ideally, this will be done within a department or key stage. Very recently, I delivered a session to my English faculty colleagues on teaching transactional writing. As part of the session, the teachers grappled with the writing activities I set my students. Previously, I've shown the PE department at my school how to live-model high mark exam questions in their subject, using a visualiser. If your head of department or key stage hasn't prioritised teaching writing, keep pestering them until it features on your CPD offer. What could be more useful for a group of primary school teachers to see a colleague with a geography degree talk them through the most important aspects of conveying knowledge and structuring arguments in a geographical information text? What could be more useful for a department of technology teachers than spending time discussing which sentence structures are the most useful for prompting thoughtful and incisive product evaluations?

In the meantime, as an individual, you will be keen to get working on developing how you teach writing. You'll want to know a few key things that will make a big difference to the quantity and quality of writing of the boys in your class. I'm going to give you some specific examples during the rest of this chapter. But, to begin with, here are three central areas to focus on. If you only change three things about how you teach boys to write, make it these.

Improving boys' writing tip 1: Take them through each stage of the writing process

As Chapter 6 illustrated, modelling is essential for increasing challenge and demystifying the writing process. Aim to live-model writing for a part of each lesson, deconstructing each writing strategy that you introduce to boys. All leaders need to ensure that all teachers are supported in using this foundational pedagogical tool.

Teaching boys how to take notes effectively, for example, is something that most teachers neglect to do, assuming that boys will somehow just *know* how to do it. I had some insight into how younger boys approach note-taking during my recent disastrous attempts to homeschool my primary-aged children during lockdown. I had asked them to read a long text about Stonehenge but because I hadn't been explicit about effective annotation, and hadn't asked them to use synonyms, they simply, and understandably, just copied down chunks of the text.

Similarly, I recently mentored a very smart year 12 boy who had no idea how to annotate the academic reading materials that I'd given him to read. Only after I went through my method, did he really understand the benefits of using an organised approach to note-taking. Here's an example of annotations about the character of Emilia in *Othello*, which I modelled to him:

Ask Mrs. R who this is and where I can find a copy

Find exact quotation from the text. IMPORTANT for betrayal essay

Traditionally, directors have depicted Emilia as a plain character, looking old enough to be Desdemona's mother. According to E.A.G Honigmann, this is a mistake; Emilia should be placed in her mid-twenties and must be attractive enough to lend plausibility to Iago's theory that she has been unfaithful to him with Othello. Either way, it's clear that she is unhappily married. In Cinthio's novella (the original source), Emilia is aware of Iago's plot but is too scared of her husband's wrath to intervene. Shakespeare's Emilia probably keeps quiet about the missing handkerchief for similar reasons. It might also be argued that Emilia is a wife in denial, preferring to avoid being privy to Iago's machinations for fear of what she might discover. As we discover at the play's finale, Emilia has good reason to be wary of her violent, misogynistic husband.

Add this vocab to my flashcards. It means 'being aware of Iago's scheming'

Link to Kiernan Ryan's comments about misogyny in Venice

Remember though, that note-taking skills are specific to each subject. So, think carefully about how note-taking works best in the subject you teach and *share this procedure repeatedly* with your students.

Improving boys' writing tip 2: Focus on word, sentence and whole-text level

The recent EEF report Improving Literacy in Secondary Schools noted that:

> There is evidence to suggest that by focusing on the micro-elements of writing for longer, students will ultimately be able to write longer, high quality responses.[19]

What might this kind of instruction look like in your lessons?

○ Word-level

You could develop boys' vocabulary through repeated exposure to synonyms, complete with precise definitions.

For example, they could improve their writing using alternative **analytical verbs** to replace 'suggests' or 'shows':

Illustrates	creates a distinct image
Implies	suggests something beyond the obvious
Highlights	draws clear attention towards by making it stand out
Evokes	brings about a strong feeling or idea
Reiterates	repeats or supports the same point/feeling/idea
Insinuates	makes a vague suggestion beyond the obvious meaning
Advocates	puts forwards a particular opinion/viewpoint/belief
Reveals	makes a meaning/interpretation clear that was previously unclear

Or you could provide a list of helpful **evaluative verbs** with synonyms:

Criticises	rebukes, admonishes, chastises, lambasts, castigates, demonises, condemns
Questions	queries, disputes, interrogates, examines, challenges, exposes
Ridicules	mocks, trivialises, satirises, lampoons, derides, parodies, caricatures
Celebrates	commemorates, recognises, acknowledges, memorialises, elevates, glorifies
Subverts	undermines, overturns, alters, modifies, corrupts
Accepts	welcomes, embraces, affirms, reaffirms

○ **Sentence level**

To improve boys' academic prose, you could show them how to use more complex sentence structures. You might, for example:

Show them how to use **appositives**, a noun or noun phrase that renames the noun next to it, to provide additional information.

Tavistock in Devon is a popular tourist spot in the summer months.

*Tavistock in Devon, **a small town which is located on the edge of the Dartmoor National Park,** is a popular tourist spot in the summer months.*

According to latest estimates methane is responsible for roughly 20% of global warming.

*According to latest estimates methane, **a colourless, odourless and highly flammable gas,** is responsible for roughly 20% of global warming.*

○ **Whole-text level**

Spending time showing boys how to structure their writing in a logical way is very important. For example, you might illustrate how to structure a history text using a **chronological sequence**:

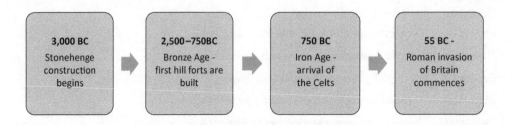

And in a future lesson, you might model how to structure a text about meat-free diets using a **sequence of importance**:

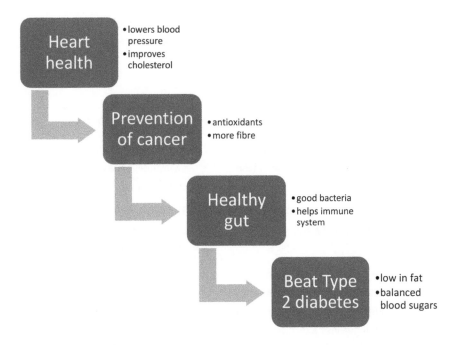

Alternatively, you might put together a checklist of things to be covered in a paragraph. Done well, this could encourage boys to write better at word, sentence and whole-text level:

Sustainability introduction checklist

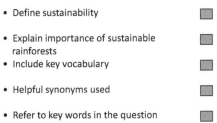

- Define sustainability

- Explain importance of sustainable rainforests
- Include key vocabulary

- Helpful synonyms used

- Refer to key words in the question

Improving boys' writing tip 3: Explicitly teach subject-specific writing techniques

So far, I've given you some generic examples of techniques to promote excellent academic writing. Yet each subject has its own academic writing 'code'. As a secondary subject expert, or a master-of-all-trades primary school teacher, it's your job to show students how to crack this code. Given that boys tend to resist, or struggle with, the more intricate aspects of academic writing in your subject, it's all the more important that you come up with a plan to tackle these issues.

You'll also need to show boys what other generic aspects of academic writing look like in the subject you teach. Let's look at the use of **discourse markers** for example:

Subject	Too informal	Appropriate formality
P.E.	*So what happens is* the swimmer gets faster through the water.	*As a result of this training*, the swimmer increases speed through the water.
Design Technology	*Something to think about* is what it could be made out of.	*The first significant consideration* when designing a product is the most suitable materials.
Biology	*The problem is that* the more cigarettes you smoke the more damage to your lungs, meaning you'll get less exercise.	*As a group*, regular smokers exercise less frequently. *A consequence of this is that* they face an increasing likelihood of cardiovascular disease.

Nominalisation – where verbs or other words (usually involving actions or descriptions) are turned into nouns (things or concepts) – is another important ingredient of successful academic writing. Here are a few examples of how nominalisation might be modelled in different subjects:

Subject	Before nominalisation	After nominalisation
Geography	One reason why carbon dioxide has gone up is because there are more *trees being cut down* so they *can't take in* as much CO_2 from the atmosphere.	A direct consequence of *deforestation* is an increase in CO_2 levels. Trees contribute to the *absorption* of CO_2, so cutting them down results in higher levels of the gas in the atmosphere.
History	The Archduke Franz Ferdinand *was killed* in June 1914. This led to the First World War *breaking out*.	The *assassination* of Archduke Franz Ferdinand in June 1914 led to the *outbreak* of the First World War.
Religious Education	Christians often meet in small groups to *study the Bible*. By doing this they can *share what they learn with each other*.	Christians often meet in small group to practise *Bible study*. By doing this they can come to a *shared understanding about Christian teachings*.

How to write like a…

In primary school, a boy might spend one lesson writing a story, full of figurative language and descriptions of a bucolic landscape. Next lesson, he's being asked to write a science report, a type of text far removed from what he's just been working on. The same happens in secondary school, but this time the boy has to contend with different teachers expecting him to write in the correct way for their subject. The aforementioned EEF literacy report found that:

> a common theme running through effective forms of writing instruction is that they support students to break down complex writing tasks and help students to become fluent in as many of the processes involved in writing as possible.[20]

Unless shared and modelled, esoteric academic writing codes overwhelm boys who are already averse to putting pen to paper. In order to want to write in your lesson, they'll need to succeed at *writing in your subject*. So, you'll need to reinforce the explicit demands of writing like a geographer, a historian, a scientist, a literary critic or a graphic designer. Here's some examples of what that might look like:

○ **Writing a lab report like a proper scientist**

Here's an example of how scientists write. Unlike in other subjects, we scientists tend to avoid the first person, using a detached and objective tone instead. What does this mean? Well, rather than writing:

> I think the plants that we are growing near the window will grow faster than the ones that are near Mr Smith's desk because there is more light there.

We will write:

> I think the pPlants that we are growing will grow faster near the a window will grow faster than the ones plants that are near Mr Smith's desk in a darker part of a room because there is more light there.

Now that's better, but it requires more precise science terminology. The hypothesis doesn't explain specifically why the lights will make the plants grow more quickly.

> …because there is more light there for photosynthesis.

The method must be described clearly and precisely, because our method must be repeatable. So instead of:

> I put 25 ml of acid into a beaker

A scientist will write:

~~I put~~ Using a measuring cylinder, put ~~25 ml~~ 25 cm^3 of ~~acid~~ H_2CO_3 into a beaker

○ **Using sentence structures to analyse historical sources like a historian**

Analysing sources is a central part of a historian's role. To be able to write like a historian, our analysis will need to show that we have gained a deeper understanding of the sources we have looked at. Here are a few sentence structures that can help with this. As with the other techniques, we will have to first model their use.

At first glance Source _ gives an impression of..., but when we look more closely at the writer's tone, we recognise that...

A similar structure we can use to show we are aiming for deeper analysis is:

On the surface..., but beneath the surface we can infer...'

○ **Structuring essay paragraphs like a social scientist**

Last lesson, I gave you the following paragraph opening sentences:

The question of ... is an emotive and controversial topic. Some groups/ commentators/theorists argue that.... For example, one of the main advocates of this view contends that... '_____'. This viewpoint suggests that...

Today, we'll develop that structure to include opposing perspectives:

On the other hand, however, other groups/commentators/theorists claim that... Most notably, _____ has argued that... '_____'. According to this perspective,...
In summary, Viewpoint A asserts that _____ while Viewpoint B puts forward a contrasting argument that _____.

○ **Writing an opinion piece like a journalist**

When you write essays, you have to be very measured and balanced when giving your own opinion. You might, for example, use phrases like this:

Personally, I would argue that...

Or

While I agree with _____'s central argument, it is my opinion that on the topic of _____ his/her viewpoint is inconsistent/contradictory/ unconvincing/lacking compelling evidence.

But when you write 'creative opinion' pieces – what we usually call writing to argue or writing to persuade – you need to use more interesting rhetorical techniques. You still consider opposing viewpoints, but in writing as a journalist you are expected to entertain as much as inform. Copy down my sentence on the topic of whether smoking should be completely banned:

> Smoking is seriously addictive. Nicotine causes unpleasant cravings, so once you start it's very difficult to stop.

My first effort is factually accurate but I nearly nodded off while I was writing it. It's a bit dull and dry. Let's bring in a classical allusion, using the myth about Hercules' near-impossible tasks:

> ~~Smoking is seriously addictive~~. It takes Herculean levels of willpower to overcome a serious nicotine addiction.

Now, I'm going to adapt the second sentence to develop this allusion:

> ~~Nicotine causes unpleasant cravings, so once you start it's very difficult to stop.~~ Like hacking off one of Hydra's heads only for two to grow back, you manage to go days without a cigarette then end up smoking three in half an hour.

Hopefully, these examples have given you a flavour of how modelling of disciplinary writing can give boys unparalleled insight into the writing process. Once you've lifted the lid on the dark arts of writing in your subject, you'll need to ensure that it becomes a regular fixture in your lessons.

Improving boys' writing tip 4: Create the right environment and practise every lesson

Ensuring that boys have lots of opportunities to engage in deliberate practice of writing is essential. As well as modelling, planning, composing, revising, editing and redrafting, you'll also need to provide regular guidance and diagnostic feedback.[21] Discussing common errors or misconceptions as a group can highlight the most effective writing strategies for students to try out. Then all students, but boys in particular, will need to spend a lot of time working on improving their writing technique. While rehearsing 'writing ideas' orally is an important part of the process, in the main, writing is an activity that needs to be undertaken with minimal distraction. To begin with, boys may not like spending sizeable chunks of lesson time practising independently while working in silence. Yet, to be able to hone their writing craft they will need to be able to concentrate. Remember the study from Chapter 4 that examined how noise disrupts our ability to think logically and rationally? It showed that, compared to adults, children suffer an even greater negative effect on cognitive processes.[22] If you want boys to get better at writing, you will need to ensure they can work in a peaceful classroom. As the author of the research concludes, 'limiting background noise in children's environments should be a critical priority if the goal is to create optimal learning environments'.[23]

- **Reduce the strain on working memory by having fewer lesson objectives**

Another way of impeding boys' learning is to overload them with too many things to think about during writing tasks. Writing is already a complex, plate-spinning activity before we add extra layers of challenge. As MacArthur et al. remind us:

> As children learn to write, much of their attention, that is, their working memory, is focused on transcription issues of spelling and handwriting, leaving less working memory for higher-level composing concerns.[24]

So how will they cope with this kind of writing lesson?
In today's lesson we're going to:

- Learn how to write an effective thesis statement for an English literature exam essay

- Understand how to avoid phrasal verbs in our writing

- Incorporate impressive vocabulary from our word bank

- SPaG focus: correct use of semi-colons

As an English teacher, I can appreciate why a fellow specialist would deem these important components of writing to work on in order to improve boys' writing skills. But in *one* lesson? Even the most confident student would struggle to work on all these aspects of writing at the same time.

So if your most pressing concern is getting boys to develop their answers by adding evidence from the text, don't overload their cognitive capabilities by picking up on spelling mistakes as you look at their work. You can make a note of these issues and address them in a future exercise. Do it while you're meant to be concentrating on something else and they'll lose sight of the initial aim.

- **Shift boys' writing motivation**

We saw in Chapter 1 that boys are more likely to adopt performance goals as part of an inclination towards extrinsic motivation. Unsurprisingly, this is also the case when it comes to writing. Research has shown that boys – especially those drawn towards traditional aspects of masculinity – show 'a stronger preference than girls for wanting to succeed in writing so as to display their competence'.[25] *What's the problem with writing to showcase your ability for the benefit of others?* you might ask. Well, the evidence is clear that performance goals have a significant direct negative impact on writing quality.[26] In other words, when boys are motivated to write to pass exams, for external praise or public recognition, they're less likely to write well in the long run. For this reason, trying to cajole a reluctant boy into writing another paragraph because it might mean the difference between a Grade 5 and a Grade 4[27] is unlikely to help improve his writing. Instead, we need to encourage boys, consciously or otherwise, to reject performance goals and instead adopt *mastery* goals when writing. As De Smedt et al. argue, 'tackling motivational writing challenges is of equal importance as teaching students cognitive writing strategies'.[28] An important 2001 study by Pajares and Valiante supports this viewpoint. The researchers found that when they controlled for girls' motivational beliefs, their advantages over boys 'were rendered non-significant'. Put another way, if boys could be steered towards approaching writing like girls tend to do, then they would become as proficient as girls in writing. It's vital that we get boys to see writing as a valuable activity, which can bring great satisfaction to the writer, rather than as a means to an assessment end. Indeed, research suggests that possessing writing motivation in itself can have a significant impact on the quality of text structure and coherence.[29]

To help boys work towards a mastery mindset, therefore, we need to help boys to set clear and specific goals (not all to be tackled at the same time, of course!). Their focus should be improving as a writer, measuring themselves against their previous efforts, not on trying to gain extra marks on the mark scheme.

● Explain the purpose of writing activities

A guaranteed way to annihilate boys' writing inclination is to use it as a punishment. Please don't say things like, 'I was going to show you a You Tube clip, but if you don't settle down we're going to do some writing instead'. And under no circumstances should you use writing as 'busy work'. You'll recall from Chapter 6 that keeping boys busy, by doing things like getting them to copy down learning objectives or other unnecessary information from the board, is not only a sign of low expectations, but will also lead to audible groans when you ask them to write something at length that is actually important. As Caroline Daly points out, using writing as a 'control mechanism' leads to boys becoming 'hostile towards writing'.[30]

Why copy it down?

That's not to say that copying down is fundamentally a bad thing. But unless boys can see the purpose of copying work from the board they are going to see it as a waste of considerable mental effort. According to Villalón et al., without careful application and explanation, this kind of writing will not improve boys' outcomes:

> the fact that writing is involved in performing numerous academic tasks does not automatically mean [that it] eventually leads to learning. If the tasks

assigned do not require knowledge-building, but only reproduction of content, then there may be no advantage, and possibly significant disadvantages in terms of effort...[31]

When we ask boys to copy from the board, therefore, we need to justify it as a knowledge-building activity. For example, as we saw in Chapter 1, a teacher's model paragraph can be copied from the board as a worked example to be adapted and applied to a different exam question. Or it might just be a really good idea that the teacher will refer back to in a future lesson. During class discussion I'll often say, 'I like that. Let's write that down and do something with that sentence/idea in our own work'. That way, my students know I'm not getting them to copy for the sake of it. A key selling point for writing things down is that it's going to be used by a student as part of their revision, in the form of retrieval and spaced practice.[32] As Graham et al. indicate, 'the permanence of writing makes ideas readily available for review and evaluation'.[33] But many boys won't automatically make this link. Teachers need to make explicit the reasons why they are asking boys to write things down.

'Just do it!'

This is particularly true of transactional writing in subjects like science, where the purpose and benefits of, say, writing up a practical might be far from obvious for the reluctant male writer.[34] When teachers get defensive ('Don't ask why, just do it!') or give a reason linked to a performance goal ('You need to do this so you can pass your next assessment'), it makes matters worse. Instead, as we saw from the example earlier in the chapter, teachers can make clear the knowledge-building benefits of scientific report writing:

- Learning how to communicate using different language and styles

- Helping clarify your own understanding of the process

- Making your results available for scrutiny to see if they are replicable

In other words, you need not only to explain to boys how to write like 'real scientist', you also need to explain *why* scientists write in that way. Of course, in order to reduce the cognitive load, you might choose to do things like give your students the method and ask them to focus on practising just one key element of the write-up. But whatever writing activity you use, you need to justify its purpose and the benefits it brings.

Ultimately, once boys see the importance of putting pen to paper – in terms of improving as a learner and making their writing available to others – you'll end up spending less time coercing boys into struggling with the blank page and more time refining their academic writing style.

How can I improve boys' academic writing?

STEPS TO SUCCESS

1 MODEL
Model each stage of the process

2 FOCUS
Focus on word, sentence and whole-text level

3 TEACH
Teach subject-specific techniques

4 PRACTISE
Practise regularly in a quiet environment

5 EXPLAIN
Explain the purpose of writing activities

Notes

1 Graham, S., Gillespie, A. & McKeown, D. (2013) 'Writing: importance, development, and instruction', *Reading and Writing*, 26, pp. 1–15.
2 Ok, it's a wobbly desk wedged into the corner of my spare bedroom, but 'study' sounds more authorial, doesn't it?
3 For a more detailed look at defamiliarisation, see Roberts, M. (2016) 'The art of making strange: creative writing done differently', available at: https://markrobertsteach. wordpress.com/2016/12/05/the-art-of-making-strange-creative-writing-done-differently/ (Accessed 19th June 2020).
4 Ibid.
5 For example, see Babayigit, S. (2015) 'The dimensions of written expression: language group and gender differences', *Learning and Instruction*, 35, pp. 33–41 or Troia, G.A., Harbaugh, A.G., Shankland, R.K., Wolbers, K.A. & Lawrence, A.M. (2013) 'Relationships between writing motivation, writing activity, and writing performance: effects of grade, sex, and ability', *Reading and Writing*, 26:1, pp. 17–44.
6 Berninger, V.W. & Fuller, F. (1992) 'Gender differences in orthographic, verbal, and compositional fluency: implications for assessing writing disabilities in primary grade children', *Journal of School Psychology*, 30:4, pp. 363–382.
7 Ibid. Also see Aitken, M. & Martinussen, R. (2013) 'Exploring predictors of performance on a curriculum-based measure of written expression', *Journal of Writing Research*, 4:3, pp. 281–299 and Olinghouse, N.G. (2008) 'Student- and instruction-level predictors of narrative writing in third-grade students', *Reading and Writing*, 21:1, pp. 3–26.
8 Ibid.
9 Bourke, L. & Adams. A.M. (2012) 'Is it differences in language skills and working memory that account for girls being better at writing than boys?', *Journal of Writing Research*, 3:3, pp. 249–277.
10 De Smedt, F., Merchie, E., Barendse, M., Rosseel, Y., De Naeghel, J. & Van Keer, H. (2018) 'Cognitive and motivational challenges in writing: studying the relation with writing performance across students' gender and achievement level', *Reading Research Quarterly*, 53:2, pp. 249–272.
11 Pajares, F. & Valiante, G. (2001) 'Gender differences in writing motivation and achievement of middle school students: a function of gender orientation?' *Contemporary Educational Psychology*, 26:3, pp. 366–381.
12 Graham, S., Berninger, V. & Fan, W. (2007) 'The structural relationship between writing attitude and writing achievement in first and third grade students', *Contemporary Educational Psychology*, 32:3, pp. 516–536.
13 Pajares, F. & Valiante, G. (2001) 'Gender differences in writing motivation and achievement of middle school students: a function of gender orientation?' *Contemporary Educational*

Psychology, 26:3, pp. 366–381. As evidence of this, they cite Crain, R.M. (1996) 'The influence of age, race, and gender on child and adolescent multidimensional self-concept', in Bracken, B.A. (ed.), *Handbook of Self-Concept: Developmental, Social, and Clinical Considerations*, pp. 395–420. New York: John Wiley & Sons, and Eccles, J., Wigfield, A., Harold, R. & Blumenfeld, P. (1993) 'Age and gender differences in children's self- and task perceptions during elementary school', *Child Development*, 64:3, pp. 830–847.

14 Guay, F., Chanal, J., Ratelle, C.F., Marsh, H.W., Larose S. & Boivin, M. (2010) 'Intrinsic, identified, and controlled types of motivation for school subjects in young elementary school children', *British Journal of Educational Psychology*, 80: 4, pp. 711–735.

15 Ibid.

16 Daly, C. (2002) 'Literature Search on Improving Boys' Writing', Office for Standards in Education (England).

17 Kiuhara, S.A., Graham, S. & Hawken, L.S. (2009) 'Teaching writing to high school students: a national survey', *Journal of Educational Psychology*, 101:1, pp. 136–160.

18 Beattie, A. (2007) 'Exploring the value of dialogue in improving boys' writing', *Changing English*, 14:2, pp. 161–174.

19 Education Endowment Foundation (2020) *Improving Literacy in Secondary Schools: Guidance Report*, London: Education Endowment Foundation.

20 Ibid.

21 Revisit Chapter 5 for an in-depth discussion of the most helpful types of feedback to use with boys.

22 For example Leibold, L.J., Yarnell, B.A. & Buss, E. (2016) 'Masked speech perception thresholds in infants, children, and adults', *Ear and Hearing*, 37, pp. 345–353.

23 Erickson, L. (2017) 'Background noise and classroom design', *The Learning Scientists Blog*, available at: https://www.learningscientists.org/blog/2017/9/13-1 (Accessed 23rd June 2020).

24 MacArthur, C.A. & Graham, S. (2016) 'Writing research from a cognitive perspective', in MacArthur, C.A., Graham, S. & Fitzgerald, J. (eds.), *Handbook of Writing Research* (2nd Ed.), New York: Guilford Press.

25 Ibid.

26 Troia, G.A., Harbaugh, A.G., Shankland, R.K., Wolbers, K.A. & Lawrence, A.M. (2013) 'Relationships between writing motivation, writing activity, and writing performance: effects of grade, sex, and ability', *Reading and Writing*, 26:1, pp. 17–44.

27 The difference between what is considered a 'good' and 'standard' pass.

28 De Smedt, F., Merchie, E., Barendse, M., Rosseel, Y., De Naeghel, J. & Van Keer, H. (2018) 'Cognitive and motivational challenges in writing: studying the relation with writing performance across students' gender and achievement level', *Reading Research Quarterly*, 53:2, pp. 249–272.

29 García, J. & Caso-Fuertes, A. (2004) 'Effects of a motivational intervention for improving the writing of children with learning disabilities', *Learning Disability Quarterly*, 27, pp. 141–159.

30 Ibid.

31 Villalón, R., Mateos, M. & Cuevas, I. (2015) 'High school boys' and girls' writing conceptions and writing self-efficacy beliefs: what is their role in writing performance?', *Educational Psychology: An International Journal of Experimental Educational Psychology*, 35, pp. 653–674.

32 See Chapter 4 for further details/a reminder of these effective learning strategies that boys should be taught.

33 Ibid.

34 Ibid.

Further reading

For more support with developing how you teach writing, you might want to take a look at some of the following resources:

Centre for Literacy in Primary Education (2018), *Writing in Primary Schools*, available at: https://clpe.org.uk/sites/default/files/Writing%20in%20Primary%20Schools_0.pdf

Considine, J. (2016) *The Write Stuff*, The Training Space Ltd: Kettering.

Hochman, J.C. & Wexler N. (2017) *The Writing Revolution: A Guide to Advancing Thinking Through Writing in All Subjects and Grades*, Jossey-Bass: San Francisco.

Kingsnorth, S. (2020) 'How should we teach writing in Primary Schools?', available at: https://medium.com/solomonkingsnorth/how-should-we-teach-writing-in-primary-schools-aadd2352af7

Quigley, A. (2018) *Closing the Vocabulary Gap*, Routledge: Abingdon, Oxon.

Trask, R.L. (1997) *The Penguin Guide to Punctuation*, Penguin Reference: London.

University of Bristol, 'Study Skills: Grammar and Punctuation', available at: https://www.ole.bris.ac.uk/bbcswebdav/courses/Study_Skills/grammar-and-punctuation/index.html#/id/5eafef1688d7eb04c5efb3dc

Webb, J. (2020) *Teach Like A Writer: Expert Tips on Teaching Students to Write in Different Forms*, John Catt: Woodbridge.

8   What can I do to get boys reading?

What's the issue?

Across the globe, boys underperform compared to girls in reading literacy measures. In their report on the 2018 PISA[1] tests, which focus on students aged 15, the Organisation for Economic Co-operation and Development (OECD) defined reading literacy as 'understanding, using, evaluating, reflecting on and engaging with texts in order to achieve one's goals, to develop one's knowledge and potential, and to participate in society'.[2] In other words, students who struggle to read effectively do less well than their peers academically. They also struggle to succeed later in life. In each of the countries that took part in the 2018 PISA reading tests, girls significantly outperformed boys. Often this was by an average of approximately 30 points, which equates to the equivalent of nearly a school year of progress.[3]

If we look at reading frequency, the same 2018 PISA report, found that:

> When asked how much time they usually spend reading for enjoyment, more than 75% of boys reported either none at all or less than 30 minutes a day; less than 3% reported that they read more than two hours a day. By contrast, 43% of girls reported that they read at least 30 minutes a day, and 8% of them reported reading more than 2 hours a day.

Very recently, a report called 'Children and young people's reading in 2020 before and during the COVID-19 lockdown', which was undertaken by the UK's National Literacy Trust,[4] reported similarly worrying figures about boys' reading habits in comparison to girls':

● The gap in reading enjoyment (the respective percentages of boys and girls who say they enjoy reading) 'widened from 2.3 percentage points at the beginning of 2020 to 11.5 percentage points during lockdown'

● The gap in daily reading (the respective percentages of boys and girls who say they read each day) increased from 4.3 percentage points at the start of the year to 7.4 percentage points during the lockdown

To summarise, we were already confronted with stark worldwide figures: boys read less well and less often, leading frequently to academic underperformance. Now, to make matters worse, the pandemic – in the UK at least but presumably elsewhere – has magnified this pre-existing gender gulf. Faced with such stark figures, we might be tempted to ascribe these gender reading differences to boys having some form of natural deficit that leaves them less skilled at reading, and less keen to read as a result. But *is* there any evidence for biological explanations of the gender reading gap? Are boys predisposed to find reading more of a struggle than girls?

Are differences in reading literacy best explained by biological or cultural factors?

Researchers, such as Clements et al., who used a phonological task where participants had to say whether two 4-letter nonsense words rhymed, found some evidence that 'males are more left lateralised on language tasks and females are more right lateralised on visuospatial tasks'.[5] A different response to these visual phonological stimuli could theoretically explain reading differences by gender. Yet, at the same time, Clements et al. acknowledge that the findings of other brain image studies 'are inconsistent', particularly when involving different reading tasks, such as involving comprehension, which 'have produced conflicting results'.

As it stands, MRI scans and other scientific advances have *not* yet provided any clear explanation for secondary-aged boys' poorer reading scores compared to girls. Furthermore, when we delve into the body of research that shows that there is little difference between the reading performance of year 1 and year 2 boys and girls,[6] claims that nature plays a bigger part than nurture start to look shaky. Indeed, Limbrick et al.'s 2012 research[7] into year 1 and year 2 pupils in Australia led them to highlight the influence of factors other than 'raw' reading ability:

> There may be no real differences between boys and girls in reading initially, but significant difference in *behaviour* between boys and girls, and teacher responses to behaviour,[8] can result in different academic outcomes over time.

Boys as 'weaker readers'

Teachers' assumptions about boys and reading, rather than their actual reading potential, go some way towards explaining the large amount of research that suggests that boys are more likely to have reading disabilities than girls. Wheldall et al.'s research, for example, which accessed a sample of over a million 8-year-olds and 10-year-olds, found that while more boys than girls experience reading problems, such as issues with decoding and fluency, 'these differences in incidence may be more modest than previous research has suggested'.[9] In explaining the discrepancy between previous studies that found much larger male to female ratios of struggling readers, Wheldall et al. point to the likelihood of 'referral bias', where teachers place 'an overemphasis on identifying boys with reading difficulties, because it is assumed that there will be far more boys than girls with reading difficulties'. Put simply, knowing that older primary age boys are a bit more likely to struggle with reading means that teachers are more likely to refer large numbers of them for remedial support. In addition, as Limbrick et al. illustrates, the behaviour of some boys means they are more likely to be identified as having a reading disability.

The million word question

Instead of thinking in terms of genetic influences, we need to look further at how boys' attitudes to reading – and their teachers' responses to these attitudes – impact on their outcomes. We need to consider how their reading motivation, or rather lack of it, is thwarting their academic potential. For example, a 2012 study of primary school children aged 8–11, conducted by McGeown et al., found 'no sex differences in reading skill'. Instead, they confirmed that 'girls had significantly higher intrinsic reading motivation'.[10] A very recent meta-analysis of studies investigating the links between motivation and reading, which scrutinised data from over 690,000 students, had findings that were:

> consistent with past literature that has reported that intrinsic motivation is positively associated with reading in samples from preschool through high school grades.[11]

You'll recall from Chapter 1 that when students are intrinsically motivated to succeed at academic activities – i.e. they want to do something for the inherent satisfaction it brings, rather than for external rewards or recognition – they are far more likely to achieve their aims. When we discuss students and reading, our ultimate wish is for them to 'read for pleasure'. Or to put it another way, we want them to read for the sheer enjoyment of it, rather than because they feel obliged to navigate their way through texts because there is no other choice. That's the difference between intrinsic and extrinsic reading motivation; and research consistently shows that girls are significantly more likely to possess intrinsic reading motivation. But our understandable desire to get boys reading for the love of it raises a $64,000 question. In fact, no. Let's call it a 1,000,000 word question: *how exactly are we meant to get boys who can't stand the idea of even picking up a book to make the leap and become keen and regular readers?* We'll return to this key question later in the chapter. For now, we need to consider why boys lack that intrinsic motivation in the first place. Why do many boys see reading as a frustrating inconvenience while girls are much more likely to view it as a pleasurable distraction?

Reading is for girls

As with writing, there is a pervasive stereotypical perception that reading is a feminine activity. As McGeown et al. note,[12] citing the research of Elaine Millard:[13]

> From an early age, reading is recognised within the home environment as an activity more closely associated with females than males. For example, when questioned on their home environment, children report that their mothers read more than their fathers, and that their mothers played a more significant role in teaching them to read.

Yet McGeown et al. make a crucial point about sex differences and reading. If we want to understand boys' reading ability, and why they tend not to like reading, we need to think in terms of gender identity, and gender conformity, rather than biological sex. Boys don't reject reading because they are 'naturally' inferior readers; at some point in their primary or early-secondary schooling they eschew reading because it makes them appear 'girly', leaving them vulnerable to the alienating effects of peer pressure.[14] As a result they fall behind and become further disinclined to read for enjoyment. McGeown et al.'s distinction between boys' reading skill and intrinsic reading motivation helpfully summarises this point:

> While reading may be regarded as a more feminine activity or academic subject,[15] it appears that it is not reading ability as such which is associated with more feminine traits, but rather being motivated to read.

Indeed, research from 2006, conducted by Topping et al., found that where boys possessed intrinsic reading motivation and managed to read as much as girls, to the same level of accuracy, 'boys and girls achieved similar gains, suggesting gender-specific patterns were not immutable'.[16] In other words, boys lagging behind girls in reading can be best explained by how boys *feel* about reading, rather than genetic ability. Where boys read frequently and fastidiously, they do as well as girls on reading literacy tests.

Teachers' gender stereotypes about reading

As we have seen, there is little viable evidence of deterministic gender differences in reading ability. Instead, reading gaps can be explained be boys' avoidance of reading, fuelled by stereotypes about feminine and masculine activities.

Most concerning of all, teachers – people like you and me who are paid to help them learn and reach their full potential – are contributing heavily to boys' negative beliefs about their reading ability.

When teachers believe that boys are weaker and less interested readers, the impact can be catastrophic. And this can occur from a surprisingly early age. A 2015 study into preschool teachers' attitudes about gender and reading, by Wolter et al., found that:

> The more traditional the gender role attitudes of the preschool teachers... the less were boys motivated to learn to read while in preschool and the poorer they performed on a reading skill test one year later in primary school... In contrast, girls' reading related motivation was the same, irrespective of how their preschool teachers thought about gender roles.[17]

Early absorption of stereotypes

Other studies confirm that children do become aware of common gender stereotypes from as early as 2–3 years old.[18] With increasing age, they become even more attuned to stereotypes, and begin to express traditional beliefs themselves.[19] Given the research showing the effect of primary teachers' preconceptions about boys and reading, it is unsurprising that boys absorb these beliefs. Upadyaya and Eccles' 2014 work,[20] for example, found that primary school teachers rate boys as having better maths ability than girls, but also believe that girls try harder than boys in reading. Explicitly or implicitly, these views feed into to girls' less confident views of themselves as mathematicians and boys' negative attitudes towards their reading ability.

Little wonder then that by the time boys reach adolescence they are likely to hold an entrenched view that reading is for girls. Recent research by Retelsdorf et al. involving over 1500 secondary school students from Germany, for example, found that where 'teachers reported high scores for gender stereotypes' about reading, boys viewed their reading ability less confidently.[21] According to Aronson and Steele's 2005 research, teachers who believe stereotypes about gender and reading ability 'tend to make remarks or to behave in ways that make these stereotypes more salient in class'.[22] So what might this look like in a typical classroom?

The teacher:

- asks more girls than boys to read aloud

- quickly corrects boys who make errors while reading aloud, but gives girls more opportunity to self-correct

- acts surprised when a boy chooses reading over another activity

- encourages boys to spend break time outside, while allowing girls to stay indoors

- nudges boys and girls towards different genres and types of texts

- starts boys off with lower reading age material compared to girls

- uses simplified or abridged texts because they believe boys won't cope with more complex or longer texts

When teachers endorse and propagate stereotypes about gender and reading – unconsciously or not – boys pick up on it and, over time, internalise the belief that girls just read more and are better readers.

So, to summarise, when we look at the research picture around boys and reading we find that:

1. Boys generally perform less well than girls on reading tests

2. Boys read less frequently and enjoy reading less than girls, and this enjoyment gap has widened during the 2020 pandemic

3. The gender gap is much better explained by cultural attitudes towards reading than any biological differences

4. When boys' negative attitudes towards reading are controlled for, gender reading gaps disappear

5. Teachers hold stereotypical preconceptions about boys' reading ability and, from an early age, boys pick up on this

Armed with this evidence, it's clear that we need to get boys reading often and reading for enjoyment. This will ensure they do as well as girls on reading tests. Identifying the remedy is easy. But, in practice, shifting boys' mindsets is going to be difficult. Let's start to look at some steps we can take to make a start on this colossal task...

What can we do about it?

● **Challenge stereotypes about boys and reading**

Despite the small sample size, the research of Pansu et al.[23] offers some evidence that when teachers' stereotypical attitudes about boys and reading are taken out of the equation, gender reading gaps can evaporate. In conditions where stereotypes about gender and reading were reduced 'boys and girls performed similarly'. Interestingly, in the groups that were subjected to stereotypes about gender and reading, the negative effects on boys' reading were observed even when the stereotypes were 'subtle and implicit' as opposed to 'explicit and directional'. In other words, teachers don't even need to make obvious, blatantly stereotypical comments to have a damaging impact on boys' views of themselves as readers. It's essential, therefore, that we think very carefully about the language we use and decisions we make. Think about what you might say, for example, in the following scenarios:

● Abdul wants to move up to purple books but you're not sure whether he's quite ready

● Mr Jameson sticks his head into your classroom and asks if you can recommend any good books about football for Billy, explaining that he's mad about sport but not a keen reader

- Your head of department asks you to re-write the scheme of learning, as there are a few 'boy-heavy' classes and they're likely to struggle with that much reading

- You lend Connor an action adventure book based on Greek myths and he brings it back the next day saying he read a few pages but didn't enjoy it

- Angus, who is notorious for rushing through his maths questions, says he has finished and wants to read his book while everyone else completes the test

There isn't necessarily an obvious answer to these situations. Context is all-important. But how you react to scenarios like these will send out powerful messages to the colleagues you work with and the boys that you teach.

- **Don't just rely on DEAR**

There is no shortage of initiatives that are designed to ensure that boys have sufficient independent reading opportunities in school. When I was at middle school, we had USSR (Uninterrupted Sustained Silent Reading). When I moved to my second school as Head of English, I inherited a reading practice that is popular among many schools: DEAR (Drop Everything And Read). Regardless of what lesson students were in, be it English or textiles or PE, they would simply read for 30 minutes. While a noble, well-intentioned scheme, I quickly spotted the programme's serious limitations. Boys who liked reading grasped the chance to make a further dent into their latest book. Boys who disliked reading did all they could to avoid reading: constant requests to go to the toilet, or change their book (for the fourth time that week), or enquiring whether they might possibly read on their phone instead, as they found that 'easier'. For struggling and reluctant male readers, DEAR had quickly mutated into DEAPR (drop everything and *pretend* to read). If I'd been given a quid for every time I spotted a boy 'reading' *Diary of a Wimpy Kid* upside down, I'd have had enough money to buy a signed first edition of *His Dark Materials*.[24] Far from closing reading gaps, DEAPR was unwittingly accentuating them. As Alex Quigley notes:

> We should critically appraise such important choices with our precious curriculum time. The research evidence that attends sustained silent reading can prove variable in its impact on our pupils' reading...[25]

Quigley cites the findings of a 2019 EEF literacy report that found that silent reading initiatives have 'inconsistent effects on student outcomes and motivation'.[26] Some schools have implemented DEAR with great success. But these positive outcomes have only happened when DEAR has been used in conjunction with other motivational strategies. Unless you design reading interventions that not only provide boys with the time to read but also chip away at their anti-reading mindsets, your silent reading programmes will be doomed to perpetuate the gender reading gap.

● **Create and maintain a whole-school reading culture**

CASE STUDY 1

Alice Visser-Furay, reading intervention specialist, literacy coordinator, English and History teacher, King Alfred's Academy, Oxfordshire

Boys don't read? At King Alfred's Academy, they do…

We are a large mixed comprehensive in rural Oxfordshire with an increasing number of disadvantaged students, largely from white working-class backgrounds; boys make up 52% of the year 7–11 cohort.

Several years ago we didn't have any sort of reading culture. The library for year 7 and 8 was used for detentions and meetings; the stock was outdated and the environment unwelcoming. Even within the English department, there was little talk about the importance of reading for pleasure. Teachers and leaders had no idea about the reading progress – or lack thereof – of our students as we did not test or evaluate students' reading. No interventions were in place, except putting students in boy-heavy bottom sets which had a negative impact on behaviour and progress. When asked about reading at King Alfred's, one year 7 boy said 'they don't give us help with reading, and if you can't read by yourself because you struggle, then you won't improve on any reading.'

We are delighted that over the course of only 4 years, we have managed to build a reading culture and transform boys' reading attitudes and attainment. The following information comes from the Accelerated Reader (AR) programme, which we started using in 2016, and from opinion surveys.

■ In the 2019–2020 school year, 58% of our 94 'Word Millionaires' were boys. Word millionaire status is achieved through the AR programme. Each time a student passes a quiz on a book they have read, they are 'awarded' the total word count of the book

■ Between Oct 2019 and January 2020, year 7 boys made on average 5 months reading age progress, compared to 3 months for the whole cohort

■ In 2019–2020, 95% of year 7 and 8 boys engaged with Accelerated Reader quizzing (100% in 2018–2019)

■ In 20182019, 68% of year 7 and 8 boys reported reading more than they had in primary school

■ Previously struggling/reluctant male readers report that that they feel 'motivated' and 'encouraged' by our approaches to reading. 'I used to think I hated reading, but then Miss helped me find interesting books. Now I love it' said one boy; another commented that 'I thought reading was really hard and hardly ever finished books. Now after help from Reading Partners in year 7, I feel much more confident – I even became a word millionaire in year 8!'

How did we achieve this turnaround? First and foremost, we have worked on improving our library to ensure it is a dynamic and welcoming space with a wide range of books to interest all students. We create and regularly update booklists with recommendations for age-appropriate books in different genres. We focus particularly on books to engage reluctant and struggling readers, investing in Barrington Stoke and Badger Learning books which are dyslexia-friendly or short and engaging. We buy heavily discounted books from charity shops, and add them to the library, sell them at parents' evenings or gift them to Pupil Premium students, knowing that book ownership plays a role in reading engagement. In 2018–2019, 3210 books were donated or sold to our students!

Another key factor is the implementation of a whole school reading policy which is strongly supported by the Senior Leadership Team and the larger KA's community. Every student is expected to have a book with them at all times, and this is checked by teachers throughout the day. Students who don't have a book are sent to the library to receive personalised advice on book choice. All English lessons in Key Stage 3 begin with 10 minutes of silent reading, and many other subjects choose to begin their lessons with reading also. We communicate regularly with parents about our whole school reading policy, emphasising the importance of reading and ensuring that they know how to encourage and support a child who is a reluctant reader. We use parents' evenings for book-tailored advice and book sales.

The Accelerated Reader (AR) programme has underpinned our reading turnaround, as it helps us to monitor progress and put in place interventions where needed – and we have also found it beneficial for improving engagement with reading. Some argue that AR only leads to superficial or extrinsic motivation, but we have found that the consistency of regular reading and quizzing builds stamina, which leads to higher motivation and engagement as students begin to see themselves as readers. Over time, we have learned to use the AR programme effectively:

- We have dedicated AR silent reading lessons once per fortnight run exclusively by teachers with a strong interest in young people's fiction. These teachers regularly check students' reading engagement through their quizzing records, AR books and one-to-one discussions

- Students are encouraged to quiz on books that are the right level of challenge for them – though we certainly don't restrict students from reading books that their test results say are 'too hard'

- The most recalcitrant readers are flagged and given individual support by the Reading Intervention Specialist

- Success is celebrated: we contact home for students who have shown improved engagement; from 2018–2020, we had 121 boy word millionaires

- Students take Star Reading Tests four times per year. They receive a label with their Standardised Score (they know to try to get to 100 or higher). We don't share reading ages with students as this can be demoralising for weaker readers

Because of our regular testing, we are able to put timely interventions in place. We are particularly thrilled with the impact of the 'Reading Partner' programme (started in

2018). Students with a low reading age are given weekly one-to-one 30-minute reading sessions with trained community volunteers; most of the volunteers are retired and it is heartwarming to see the grandparent/child relationship that develops, giving students a positive experience of reading. In 2019–2020, 14 (out of 23) year 7 students receiving this intervention were boys – and this group of boys made a stunning 20 months of progress in 3 months! In 2018–2019, 20 of 24 year 7 'Reading Partner' students were boys, and they made an average 19.7 months of progress over the course of 8 months.

We have also started a 'Reading Scholar' programme for struggling Pupil Premium Key Stage 3 and 4 students, which included lots of boys; plus a 'Link Leaders' programme for year 8 boys with significant behaviour issues (often linked with poor literacy). Both of these interventions involve trained members of staff doing Academic Reading in small groups using research-driven Reciprocal Reading strategies.

Finally, we have many reading events throughout the year to generate a buzz around reading – and we actively recruit boys to participate. These include Carnegie Shadowing (28 boys participated in 2019, including several previously reluctant readers); Read for Empathy initiatives; World Book Day celebrations; Summer Reading Bingo challenges; Library Leader roles; and an afterschool Library Elective programme, which had 10 students in 2019–2020 – all boys!

● Provide boys with easy access to books to read at home

As Visser-Furay highlights, we know from research into reading and achievement that having access to books at home is linked to educational success.[27] We also know, however, from a 2018 National Literacy Trust survey that 'more girls than boys say that they have a book of their own at home, and the difference is statistically significant'.[28] The survey goes on to illustrate that when these boys are FSM or have SEN status, the likelihood of them owning books at home lessens further. Parents are more likely to give a book as a present to a daughter than to a son. In schools like King Alfred's, where the library is prioritised as a focal point for all learners, boys still have access to high quality reading material. But elsewhere libraries are closing at a worrying rate, both in schools and in wider communities. As Nonte et al.'s recent research argues:

> School libraries, especially if they are well equipped, have been strongly linked to both positive attitudes toward reading and student reading achievement...[29]

Where school libraries are closed or poorly-stocked, some dedicated classroom teachers have seized the initiative and plugged the gaps, making books available for boys to take home and read.

As Freya Odell writes on her blog,[30] finding out more about reading interests and setting up a classroom library was without doubt the most successful strategy she has used to boost boys' engagement with reading.

CASE STUDY 2

Freya Odell, Head of English, St George's British International School, Rome

A really influential book for me was *The Book Whisperer* by Donalyn Miller. One of her first recommendations was that in order for students to read we need to capture their interest. She says:

> In order to make personal reading recommendations to my students, I need to learn about their past reading experiences and their interests both in and out of school. I mine these surveys for nuggets of information that will form the basis for book recommendations. Students may not be able to describe what types of books they might like to read, but if I have knowledge of their personal interests, I will be able to find books that match a topic they enjoy.[31]

I issued my students with an interest survey and it was really interesting to 'mine' these surveys and find out more about my students' interests, hobbies and ideas.

Miller suggests that you build your own classroom library for your own classroom. After reading this, I bought everyone in the department a bookshelf and promised more bookshelves when those ones had been filled up. I filled my bookshelf up.

One day the magic happened. A student stayed behind after the lesson to ask if they could borrow one of my books and take it home to read. We forget that statistics have said that there are many families without a single book in their house, increasing the importance of libraries. I was delighted. And soon after, another student asked to borrow a book and then another. One boy's mum apologised after she found about five books at their home!

Now every time I buy a new book for the library, I make sure I read it first and then I spend five minutes of that lesson telling them about that book and sharing excerpts with them. I recently did this with *One* by Sarah Crossan[32] and Robin Talley's *Lies We Tell Ourselves*.[33] The next lesson, students made a beeline for the book. And then I realised that some students had been to the school library to take this book out. And then I realised that some students had asked their parents to buy the book. So the importance with the classroom library is that each book that goes on to the shelf has been read and recommended by you.

● **Reject myths about boys' reading preferences**

Despite Odell's success with getting boys hooked on novels from the classroom library, generally, girls like reading fiction, while boys prefer non-fiction. Right? Well, while some researchers have argued[34] that there is evidence to suggest that given a choice boys do opt for non-fiction, others have outlined a more nuanced view of boys' reading habits. Recent research by Margaret Merga, for example, which examined the reading preferences of Australian children, showed that 'male respondents...displayed no marked preference for non-fiction, and males were more likely to prefer to exclusively read fiction than non-fiction'.[35]

Using a much smaller sample of three year 6 classrooms, Moss and McDonald's intriguing 2004 study[36] found that boys borrowed as much fiction as the girls and that 'non-fiction made up only 10% of the stock borrowed'. As Moss and McDonald explain, the widespread belief that boys want or need a diet comprised mainly of non-fiction, despite the evidence for this assertion being mixed at best, taps into a common perception that school libraries are too feminised and 'do not do enough to supply or promote the kinds of non-fiction that boys are really interested in'. In reality, Moss and McDonald contend:

> the boys most likely to choose to read non-fiction texts during quiet reading time were those whom the school designated 'weak readers'. The kinds of non-fiction texts they chose were from a highly specific subset that were both visually dense and deployed non-linear reading paths.

The non-fiction picture book

In other words, boys' apparent fondness for non-fiction may, in some cases, have more to do with the type of non-fiction 'picture books' that struggling male readers are encouraged to pick up during reading time. Indeed, where Moss and McDonald found boys reading fiction with enthusiasm, it was not related to the genre of books that boys were given. Instead it was down to a classroom culture that very much resembles Freya Odell's classroom; one that encouraged and enabled books to be shared between children:

> ...it is about creating the opportunities for children to circulate texts amongst themselves more informally. This is both about having enough of the same texts available to allow for this kind of sharing (a single copy of a popular book would make it harder to circulate), but also about creating the space for children to be able to recommend texts to each other so that what has been borrowed and what is worth spending time on becomes visible and common knowledge, in an appropriate forum.

● **Investigate the potential of audiobooks**

Remember those depressing figures from the start of the chapter about boys' reading during lockdown? Well, not everything contained in the report about boys and books is so dire. One area of particular interest to teachers trying to chip away at gender reading gaps is the potential of audiobooks to get boys engaged with stories. As the authors of the report point out, audiobooks are 'the only format where more boys than girls said that they enjoy it more and are doing it more often'.[37]

Intriguingly, audiobooks appear to act as something of a 'gateway drug' for getting boys hooked on to other forms of reading, with 51.1% of boys 'saying that listening to audiobooks has increased their interest in reading'. There may well be other literacy benefits: 43.2% of boys reported that listening to audiobooks 'has made them more interested in writing'.

Are audiobooks 'proper' reading?

Nonetheless, despite these promising figures, you might worry that in pushing audiobooks onto boys you'll rob them of the benefits of actually reading print. Yet as Daniel Willingham has noted 'research shows that adults get nearly identical scores on a reading test if they listen to the passages instead of reading them'.[38] Listening to books can aid elements of comprehension by allowing students to pick up on the nuances of the tone, with an emphasis on certain words. However, as Willingham explains, one study showed how readers of print outperformed listeners of podcasts on comprehension quizzes performed two days later, scoring 81 percent compared to 59 percent.[39] And the reason for this?

> When we focus, we slow down. We reread the hard bits. We stop and think. Each is easier with print than with a podcast. Print also supports readers through difficult content via signals to organization like paragraphs and headings, conventions missing from audio...difficult texts demand additional mental strategies.[40]

Audiobooks aren't a panacea then. But they certainly offer a possible route to getting more boys reading. They have practical advantages, like being able to listen to them while you exercise or get the bus to school. Get boys listening to stories and they might just be more likely to move on to print.

● **Move from extrinsic to intrinsic rewards over time**

Chapter 1 demonstrated the links between extrinsic motivation and boys' academic underperformance. As such, we view systems like Accelerated Reader that reward boys for completing quizzes, or reading a certain number of words in a year, with scepticism. By contrast, intrinsic reading motivation is widely acknowledged as a key factor in developing reading achievement among boys. I adore reading but, let's be honest, there are times when it can be a chore rather than a joyful activity. Whether it's Derrida, Dickens or *Mrs Dalloway*, I've had reading experiences less pleasurable than trips to the dentist. But I've persisted. And have gained insight and understanding along the way (ok, not with Derrida). As Froiland and Oros assert:

> Intrinsic motivation helps the reader to persist through challenging parts of texts and thus to be thoroughly engaged in reading, instead of quitting when it becomes difficult.[41]

Indeed, Froiland and Oros's research suggests that gender reading achievement gaps can disappear when intrinsic motivation is introduced. When faced with challenging reading – and for many boys we're not talking *Bleak House* but rather relatively simple texts – intrinsic motivation is essential. Something like an Accelerated Reader certificate surely isn't going to cut it. Yet, as Alice Visser-Furay's and Freya Odell's case studies illustrate, reluctant readers will need some encouragement in the early days of their transition from non-readers to regular readers. It would be a mistake to think that extrinsic influences can sustain their interest in the long run. But starting with a few innocuous extrinsic rewards, and then gradually hooking them onto the intrinsic benefits of reading for pleasure makes sense. In both case studies, we see how the right support from their teachers leads to a tipping point. To begin with, you might prompt boys to reading by insisting on certain expectations, or because they get something out of it. But if you persist and work on their intrinsic motivation you might find that, seemingly against all odds, they have become habitual readers. Once boys start to enjoy the activity of reading in itself, your work is done.

What can I do to get boys reading?

STEPS TO SUCCESS

1 **ENSURE** Ensure boys have access to high quality books

2 **CREATE** Create a buzz about certain texts

3 **IGNORE** Ignore the non-fiction myth

4 **CONSIDER** Consider audiobooks as a starting point

5 **WITHDRAW** Withdraw extrinsic rewards over time

Notes

1 Programme for International Student Assessment.
2 Schleicher, A. (2018) 'PISA 2018: insights and interpretation', Organisation for Economic Co-operation and Development, Paris: OECD. Available at: https://www.oecd.org/pisa/PISA%202018%20Insights%20and%20Interpretations%20FINAL%20PDF.pdf
3 Pansu, P., Régner, I., Max, S., Colé, P., Nezlek, J.B., & Huguet, P. (2016) 'A burden for the boys: evidence of stereotype threat in boys' reading performance', *Journal of Experimental Social Psychology*, 65, pp. 26–30.
4 Clark, C., & Picton, I. (2020) 'Children and young people's reading in 2020 before and during the COVID-19 lockdown', London: National Literacy Trust.
5 Clements, A.M., Rimrodt, S.L., Abel, J.R., Blankner, J.G., Mostofsky, S.H., Pekar, J.J., Denckla, M.B., & Cutting, L.E. (2006) 'Sex differences in cerebral laterality of language and visuospatial processing', *Brain and Language*, 98:2, pp. 150–158.
6 Such as Entwistle, D.R., Alexander, K.L., & Olson, L.S. (2007) 'Early schooling: the handicap of being poor and male', *Sociology of Education*, 80:2, pp. 114–138, McCoach, D.B., O'Connell, A.A., & Levitt, H. (2006) 'Ability grouping across kindergarten using an early childhood longitudinal study', *The Journal of Educational Research*, 99:6, pp. 339–346, and Savage, R., & Carless, S. (2004) 'Predicting curriculum and test performance at age 7 years from pupil background, baseline skills and phonological awareness at age 5', *British Journal of Educational Psychology*, 74:2, pp. 155–171.

7 Limbrick, L., Wheldall, K., & Madelaine, A. (2012) 'Reading and related skills in the early school years: are boys really more likely to struggle?', *International Journal of Disability, Development and Education*, 59:4, pp. 341–358.

8 For a detailed overview of this phenomenon, see Chapter 5 of Pinkett, M., & Roberts, M. (2019) *Boys Don't Try? Rethinking Masculinity in Schools*, Abingdon: Routledge.

9 Wheldall, K., & Limbrick, L. (2010) 'Do more boys than girls have reading problems?', *Journal of Learning Disabilities*, 43:5, pp. 418–429.

10 McGeown, S., Goodwin, H., Henderson, N., & Wright, P. (2012) 'Gender differences in reading motivation: does sex or gender identity provide a better account?', *Journal of Research in Reading*, 35:3, pp. 328–336.

11 Toste, J.R., Didion, L., Peng, P., Filderman, M.J., & McClelland, A.M. (2020) 'A meta-analytic review of the relations between motivation and reading achievement for K–12 students', *Review of Educational Research*, 90:3, pp. 420–456.

12 Ibid.

13 Millard, E. (1997) 'Differently literate: gender identity and the construction of the developing reader', *Gender and Education*, 9:1, pp. 31–48,

14 See Chapter 3 of Pinkett, M. & Roberts, M. (2019) *Boys Don't Try? Rethinking Masculinity in Schools*, Abingdon, Oxon: Routledge, for more on how peer pressure impedes boys' academic progress.

15 Dwyer, C.A. (1974) 'Influence of children's sex role standards on reading and arithmetic achievement', *Journal of Educational Psychology*, 66:6, pp. 811–816.

16 Topping, K., Samuels, J., & Paul, T. (2008) 'Independent reading: the relationship of challenge, non-fiction and gender to achievement', *British Educational Research Journal*, 34:4, pp. 505–524.

17 Wolter, I., Braun, E., & Hannover, B. (2015) 'Reading is for girls!? The negative impact of preschool teachers' traditional gender role attitudes on boys' reading related motivation and skills', *Frontiers in Psychology*, 6:1267, pp. 1–11.

18 Such as Trautner, H., Ruble, D., Cyphers, L., Kirsten, B., Behrendt, R., & Hartmann, P. (2005) 'Rigidity and flexibility of gender stereotypes in children: developmental or differential?', *Infant and Child Development*, 14:4, pp. 365–381 and Banse, R., Gawronski, B., Rebetez, C., Gutt, H., & Morton, J.B. (2010) 'The development of spontaneous gender stereotyping in childhood: relations to stereotype knowledge and stereotype flexibility', *Developmental Science*, 13:2, pp. 298–306.

19 For example, Martinot, D., Bages, C., & Desert, M. (2012), 'French children's awareness of gender stereotypes about mathematics and reading: when girls improve their reputation in math', *Sex Roles*, 66, pp. 210–219; Rowley, S.J., Kurtz-Costes, B., Mistry, R., & Feagans, L. (2007) 'Social status as a predictor of race and gender stereotypes in late childhood and early adolescence', *Social Development*, 16:1, pp. 150–168; and Kurtz-Costes, B., Rowley, S.J., Harris-Britt, A., & Woods, T.A. (2008) 'Gender stereotypes about mathematics and science and self-perceptions of ability in late childhood and early adolescence', *Merrill-Palmer Quarterly*, 54:3, pp. 386–409.

20 Upadyaya, K., & Eccles, J., (2014) 'Gender differences in teachers' perceptions and children's ability self-concepts', in *Gender Differences in Aspirations and Attainment* (eds.) Schoon, I., & Eccles, J., Cambridge University Press, pp. 79–100.

21 Retelsdorf, J., Schwartz, K., & Asbrock, F. (2015) '"Michael can't read!" Teachers' gender stereotypes and boys' reading self-concept', *Journal of Educational Psychology*, 107:1, pp. 186–194.

22 Aronson, J., & Steele, C.M. (2005) 'Stereotypes and the fragility of academic competence, motivation, and self-concept', In A.J. Elliot & C.S. Dweck (Eds.), *Handbook of Competence and Motivation* (p. 436–456), New York: Guilford Publications, cited by Retelsdorf, J.,

Schwartz, K., & Asbrock, F. (2015) '"Michael can't read!" Teachers' gender stereotypes and boys' reading self-concept', *Journal of Educational Psychology*, 107:1, pp. 186–194.

23 Ibid.

24 As of October 2020, these cost between £2500 and £4500, if anyone's feeling generous.

25 Quigley, A. (2020) *Closing the Reading Gap*, Abingdon, Oxon: Routledge, p. 165.

26 Education endowment Foundation (2019) *Improving Literacy in Secondary School*, London: Education endowment Foundation.

27 Evans, M.D.R., Kelley, J., Sikora, J., & Treiman, D.J. (2010) 'Family scholarly culture and educational success: books and schooling in 27 nations', *Research in Social Stratification and Mobility*, 28:2, pp. 171–197.

28 Clark, C., & Picton, I. (2018) *Book Ownership, Literacy Engagement and Mental Wellbeing*, London: National Literacy Trust.

29 Nonte, S., Hartwich, L., & Willems, A.S. (2018) 'Promoting reading attitudes of girls and boys: a new challenge for educational policy? Multi-group analyses across four European countries', *Large-scale Assessments in Education*, 6:5, pp. 1–22.

30 Odell, F. (2016) 'Raising the profile of reading (part 1)', 3rd July 2016, wheninromeeng. wordpress.com. Available at: https://wheninromeeng.wordpress.com/2016/07/03/ raising-the-profile-of-reading-part-1/ (Accessed 3 October 2020).

31 Miller, D. (2010) *The Book Whisperer: Awakening the Inner Reader in Every Child*, Hoboken, New Jersey: John Wiley & Sons, p.39.

32 Crossan, S. (2015) *One*, London: Bloomsbury Children's Books.

33 Talley, R. (2014) *Lies We Tell Ourselves*, London: Harper Collins.

34 Such as Millard, E. (1997) *Differently Literate: Boys, Girls and the Schooling of Literacy*, London: Falmer Press and Hall, C., & M. Coles. (1997b) 'Gendered readings: helping boys develop as critical readers', *Gender and Education*, 9, pp. 61–68.

35 Merga, M. (2017) 'Do males really prefer non-fiction, and why does it matter?', *English in Australia*, 52:1, pp. 27–37.

36 Moss, G., & McDonald, J.W, (2004) 'The borrowers: library records as unobtrusive measures of children's reading preferences', *Journal of Research in Reading*, 27:4, pp. 401–412.

37 Ibid.

38 Willingham, D. (2018) 'Is listening to a book the same thing as reading it?', *New York Times*, 8th December 2018. Available at: https://www.nytimes.com/2018/12/08/opinion/sunday/audiobooks-reading-cheating-listening.html (Accessed 3rd October 2020). The research he cites is Gernsbacher, M.A., Varner, K.R., & Faust, M.E. (1990) 'Investigating differences in general comprehension skill', *Journal of Experimental Psychology, Learning, Memory, and Cognition*, 16:3, pp. 430–445.

39 Daniel, D.B., & Woody, W.D. (2010) 'They hear, but do not listen: retention for podcasted material in a classroom context', *Teaching of Psychology*, 37:3, pp. 199–203.

40 Willingham, D. (2018) 'Is listening to a book the same thing as reading it?', *New York Times*, 8th December 2018. Available at: https://www.nytimes.com/2018/12/08/ opinion/sunday/audiobooks-reading-cheating-listening.html (Accessed 3rd October 2020).

41 Froiland, J.M., & Oros, E. (2014) 'Intrinsic motivation, perceived competence and classroom engagement as longitudinal predictors of adolescent reading achievement', *Educational Psychology*, 34:2, pp. 119–132, citing Guthrie, J.T., McRae, A., & Klauda, S.L. (2007) 'Contributions of concept-oriented reading instruction to knowledge about interventions for motivations in reading', *Educational Psychologist*, 42:4, pp. 237–250.

9 How can I make sure boys do well in creative writing?

What's the issue?

Let's begin with some statistics.

In 2019, 72% of boys met the expected standard for the Key Stage 2 writing SAT.[1] For girls the figure was 85%. In terms of pupils classified by their teachers to be working at greater depth,[2] just 15% of boys achieved this measure, compared to 25% of girls. The gender SATs achievement gap of 13 percentage points for meeting the expected standard is bigger than both reading and maths, where boys lag behind by 9 and 1 percentage points respectively.[3] It's worth noting at this stage that, unlike the reading and maths SATs, the writing SAT is teacher-assessed.

Also in 2019, in GCSE English language, 63% of boys achieved Grade 4 or above, compared to 78% of girls. The measure for Grade 7 or above was 12% of boys compared to 23% of girls.[4] Half the marks available for GCSE English language are based on creative writing tasks.

At primary and secondary level, when it comes to creative writing, boys are, as a whole, routinely outperformed by girls.

Access and empowerment

The stubborn persistence of the writing gap should be a concern to anyone working in education. Making expected progress and passing exams are important, of course. But even more important is the impact of being a confident writer on the psyche of an individual. As Debra Myhill asserts:

> Improving a child's ability to articulate thoughts, ideas and responses in writing may in part be about 'standards' but, far more than that, it is about access and empowerment.[5]

In our society, many young men struggle to gain decent qualifications and struggle to express a range of emotions.[6] Against this backdrop, effectively teaching boys creative writing could be seen not just as an academic issue but as a moral imperative.

What does creative writing in school involve?

When we use the term 'creative writing' we usually think of writing stories. And narrative and descriptive[7] writing are certainly integral elements of creative writing. Yet we also expect students to produce other types of texts. In primary, these non-fiction texts are usually called 'information texts' and can be anything from the biography of a famous sportswoman to an explanation of how seeds germinate. At secondary level, English teachers call this 'transactional writing', which focuses on getting students to write things like essays, newspaper articles or letters arguing for or against specific statement prompts. We might not always categorise this type of writing as 'creative', but much of it is really. When writing non-fiction texts, skilled writers think creatively and frequently adopt stylistic elements that we might normally associate with narrative and descriptive writing. Look back at my opening paragraphs to Chapter 7, for one such example.

For the purpose of this chapter, I'll mainly be looking at boys and 'story writing'. But feel free to adopt a similar stance to the non-fiction texts that you get boys to work on.

Do boys dislike creative writing?

As we saw in Chapter 7, boys tend to have negative attitudes about writing in general:

- It's seen as a feminine activity

- They don't enjoy planning and editing

- It's often viewed as a necessary evil – you have to do it to pass exams but it's not an enjoyable activity in itself

Some boys will also voice these opinions when they are asked to write creatively. And, yet, for many others creative writing is *less* intimidating, *less* unappealing than writing in other subjects. In her 2001 study into attitudes towards writing, Debra Myhill noted:

> A recurring theme then, even amongst underachieving boys, was that they enjoyed the creative freedom of writing in English, in direct contrast to the more functional, content-led writing encountered elsewhere in the curriculum… asserting their preference for writing that allows them a voice and imaginative freedom…[8]

For this reason, it's important that we have high expectations about boys' motivation to write creatively. Unfortunately, though, as we shall see, our response to their creative writing can often quickly stifle their enjoyment of the activity.

What kind of creative writing do teachers like?

According to the research, those who teach creative writing, such as primary teachers and teachers of secondary English, tend to place premium value on writing that is shaped by some form of personal experience. Often, for teachers, the most exalted genre of writing, fictionalised or not, is 'autobiographical writing that emphasizes personal revelation and reflection'.[9] Think of the dreaded 'what I did during the summer holidays' activity or GCSE exam-style questions that ask students to 'write about a time when you had to make a difficult choice'.

Personal revelation and reflection are important aspects of writing. I too enjoy stories that allow us to develop our understanding of the human condition, to make us ponder the emotional backdrop of our lives. But there's a danger that in focusing in on this form of prose we can end up pushing boys away from an activity that many of them would otherwise enjoy. Some researchers on writing have suggested that when teachers evaluate students' autobiographical writing they are influenced by their own 'unstated cultural definitions of the self'.[10] Put simply, a teacher who decides that good writing has something profound to say about the feelings of the writer may disregard promising writing that fails to do this.

As Linda Peterson has argued, gender plays a big part in influencing 'the topics students choose when they write...and these choices, in turn, affect their success' in producing writing that is perceived as good or effective by their teacher. When boys choose to write outside of the dominant strand of creative writing – and as we shall see, they often do reject this type of reflective writing – there is the danger that teachers in turn judge their efforts as inadequate.

What do boys enjoy writing about?

For at least five decades, researchers into gender and children's creative writing have found clear differences in how boys and girls like to write:

Boys' writing	Girls' writing
Features very little use of the first person[11]	Uses first person as a way of looking objectively at themselves[12]
Focuses more on conflict and war, featuring lot of action[13]	Tends to focus on interactions between people and relationships[14]
Often seems fascinated with the spectacular and the grotesque[15]	Is usually far less violent than boys' writing[16]
Tends towards individualism and competition[17]	Employs tropes based on collective action[18]
Is more likely to attempt humour and be influenced by film, TV, gaming narratives[19]	Tends to resemble traditional literature texts[20]

As you can see, boys have a tendency to reject the reflective staples of narrative fictions that teachers apparently hold in high esteem. For many boys, the default model of narrative writing involves blood and guts, explosions and car chases. Why is this?

First, because writing is seen as a feminine activity, creating action-packed prose can be seen as a subversion of the act itself. As Thomas Newkirk explains:

> In one sense, writing represents the choice of language over physical action; yet this choice can be mitigated by stressing action in the writing.[21]

Should we worry about boys' violent stories?

According to Newkirk, it's a simplistic mistake to assume that boys' use of violence in writing is evidence of an aggressive or vicious nature. This is because:

> violence can be mediated, viewed with humorous detachment, and appropriated for a variety of non-violent ends... Much of the violence boys like is "violence with a wink", violence that parodies itself or at least suggests its own unreality.

When we juxtapose the kind of writing teachers value and like to read with the kind of writing boys like to produce from an early age, we find a stark disconnect. And perhaps this disparity at least contributes in part to boys' poorer outcomes on teacher-assessed writing, most notably the KS2 SAT. According to 2019 data, 85% of primary school teachers are female.[22] The vast majority of secondary English teachers are also female. Most of the teachers of creative writing to boys in this country, therefore, are female. Might it be the case that, far from the assumption that boys just dislike creative writing from an early age, female teachers' literary tastes are in some way subconsciously working against boys' creative writing development instead?

Boys' writing as lesser writing

Indeed, Linda Peterson's study of first-year college students found that:

> In terms of writing qualities, males showed no deficit at rendering detail; their lower scores were due to a perceived difficulty in rendering "significance," in the capacity to reflect on the meaning of the experience.[23]

In other words, teachers of creative writing were as impressed by their male students' writing efforts in terms of style, description and narrative precision as by the work of their female students. What they were less impressed by – indeed, what led them to award fewer marks – was male students' willingness or ability to elicit some sort of deeper meaning out of their experiences. Now of course, this research is into the narrative writing of older, more advanced college students. But the same distinct gender writing patterns, and the response of their teachers, seem to be taking place at primary and secondary levels: writing focused on action and events judged as lesser writing than that containing a greater focus on reflection and meaning.

What can we do about it?

● **Practise frequently, but only after explicit instruction**

A 2012 report into the effective teaching of creative writing in the US advised that kindergarten students (the equivalent of year 1 in the UK) should spend at least 30 minutes per day on writing and writing activities.[24] Yet research conducted in 2014 found that much less time was being spent on writing than the report recommended. Where writing practice was taking place, the researchers noted that:

> Surprisingly, most of the time spent on writing instruction was spent on students writing independently rather than on teachers providing instruction.[25]

This finding was a concern, they argued, because writing experts recommend that effective teaching of writing in primary schools needs to include a balance between teacher instruction and student independent writing. Good modelling of writing will also tackle what Susan Jones describes as the 'perception that what good writers do is have good ideas and then just write them down'.[26] Just thinking of ideas and writing stuff down is not enough. In the same way that novice golfers don't get any better if all they do is play games of golf, boys won't get better at writing just by doing more of it. A teacher needs to give boys precise examples of constructing interesting clauses, in the same way that a coach would show a junior golfing hopeful how to apply backspin to a ball.

For example, using present participles to begin sentences is an excellent way of bringing structural variety to a paragraph:

● Swimming through the sewage outlet, he gagged and retched every few yards.

● Turning on the tap with my elbow, I rinsed the blood-smeared glass from my smashed fist.

● Flicking absent-mindedly through the newspaper, the man froze as he noticed who had finally been released from prison.

As well as helping boys avoid overusing sentences that start with the personal pronoun 'I', participles like these can also to add a sense of immediacy to a boy's prose.

● **Teach the nuts and bolts of writing**

For some teachers, creative writing teaching should focus primarily on the word 'creative'. *Boys will be switched off by references to present participles and technical terminology*, they argue. *I've got an English degree and nobody ever told me about fronted adverbials or antanaclasis!*

Yet, as Debra Myhill succinctly explains, giving boys a solid understanding of technical terminology demystifies the process, allowing them to take control of their own prose, and being more creative as a result:

> Thinking of creativity and crafting as opposites misses the fundamental point, that to be creative you have to be able to shape, craft and manipulate language for effect.[27]

Terminology as a springboard

Richard Andrews also argues that teachers who are confident in their knowledge of grammar, and general literary and linguistic devices, 'will be in a better position to help young writers'.[28] Roy Corden's research supports this view, finding that rather than holding boys back, precise terminology can act as a springboard for their creative thoughts:

> The use of specific literary terms helped children to clarify their thoughts... They were able to integrate the stylistic and organizational features... into their personal repertoires and use them successfully in their own writing.[29]

Tell boys about the terminology and the results will tell. You might disagree with the definitiveness of this sentence. I happen to believe it. But I also created it to show you an example of antanaclasis, the device I mentioned a few paragraphs ago. Antanaclasis is language feature where a word or phrase is repeated within a sentence, but with a different meaning each time it appears. The first 'tell' in my example means 'inform or educate', whereas the second means 'to have an impact'. It's a neat little writing trick. I sharpen my pencil and sharpen my creative powers. My point is that if I wasn't aware of the name of this figure of speech, I probably wouldn't have been able to use it.

● **But encourage fun and creative wordplay**

As Myhill et al. state, however, good grammar teaching needs to 'include authentic examples from authentic texts',[30] as opposed to dry parsing activities that will drain the enthusiasm out of any student. When we approach writing in general, experimentation with language is to be actively encouraged.

The silly name game

In my class, when writing responses to exam questions such as 'write a letter your local MP arguing for or against the use of the death penalty', I try and liven things up a bit. To showcase their verbal inventiveness to a reader, I encourage them to use irony or word play to create names that have subversive or humorous effect. These appeal to many boys' fondness for writing with comedic elements. Examples for the death penalty piece might include:

- The Rt. Hon I. Hangemhigh
- Gloria Gallows MP
- Dr. Lee-Phil Injection
- Alex Rick Chair[31]
- Sir Steven Strangler
- Cominic Dummings[32]

Battling against cliché

Another enjoyable little writing task I use involves getting students to understand how cliché is the enemy of good writing.[33] To prove this point, we do the following activities:

1. Set pupils a trap. Give them a list of unfinished similes and get them to fill in the gaps: as fast as _____, The ball went it to net like _____ etc. Watch as most pupils automatically opt for the lazy option (a cheetah, lightning, Usain Bolt; a rocket, a missile).

2. Have a conversation about why these choices are too obvious. Discuss less obvious answers.

3. Get pupils to compose fresh, original similes. Or subvert the cliché ('John ran for the bus as fast as a cheetah. Unfortunately, the cheetah he ran like was arthritic and had three legs.) Or better still, look at alternative ways to express the thought.

4. Get them to write a list of clichés on a given topic against the clock. 'Time' works well. So does 'Love'.

5. Expand this idea so they write the most trite and hackneyed love poem of all time.

6. Give them something that you've written that is of a high quality but let down by a couple of clunkers. The best thing about this is when they *continue* to notice your clichéd offerings weeks after you've moved on to another topic.

7. Talk about the difference and overlap between cliché, idiom and proverb.

8. Give them a visual stimulus and, in pairs, get them to write two openings – one full of overused phrases and one that avoids them like, ahem, the plague.

Writing bad dialogue

Writing good dialogue is notoriously tricky. So, in order to teach boys how to write good dialogue, I start by showing them what *not* to do. To start, I provide them with the following list of Ten Deadly Dialogue Sins:

1. 'Ping pong' dialogue – characters respond to dull questions or statements with equally dull responses. There is usually a repetition of words: 'Would you like to go to the cinema?' 'Yes, I'd love to go to the cinema'. This backward and forward exchange becomes interminable, worthless filler.

2. Dialogue that follows the rules of polite conversation – in real life, people interrupt, change the topic, ignore the question, stay silent. Dialogue that is too polite lacks conflict.

3. Conversations that sound like prose – dialogue shouldn't involve complete perfectly punctuated grammatical sentences. 'Fancy the cinema?' 'Go on then' is not the greatest dialogue ever but at least sounds like it's come out of a human's mouth.

4. Telling not showing – 'Do you still love me?' 'No, I don't love you anymore...' becomes the default urge when writing dialogue. It's more difficult to 'show' during conversation but worth perseverance: 'Want to go to bed now?' 'Let's watch the end of the film'.

5. Overdoing the exposition – 'I know that you went to Oxford, and got a first in Physics, but that doesn't mean I have to listen to your opinion on everything, John.'

6. Tag thesaurus – Elmore Leonard, widely acknowledged as a master of dialogue is adamant that you should never use a verb other than 'said' to carry dialogue. And that's only if it isn't clear who's speaking in the first place. Writing usually improves dramatically after getting rid of 'cried', 'shouted' and 'hesitated'.

7. Adding unnecessary adverbs – again Leonard nails this one: 'never use an adverb to modify the verb 'said'...he admonished gravely'.[34]

8. Overdoing dialect – Unless you're Irvine Welsh, it isnae wise to – likesay – use a pure rush of vernacular 'til yer reader cannae stand it nae muir, ye ken.

9. Shoddy free indirect speech – the teacher told his pupils that he was tired of the torturous summary of the conversation that went on for what seemed like

pages. Yes, he informed them, he wanted them to incorporate this to avoid unnecessary chunks of dialogue but, as he pointed out once more, he wanted them to use it sparingly.

10. Dialogue for the sake of it – I've written a hundred words of description. My page therefore now needs a bit of dialogue to break things up a touch....

Next I ask them to write some truly stinking lines of dialogue, committing as many of the ten sins as is possible. Eventually, they learn to avoid clunky speech in their stories. Be careful, however; they will inevitably pick up on some of *your* shabby dialogue in future stories.

Boys tend to love all these activities. After doing them, they start to grasp how effective writing is *writing which is obsessed with originality and inventiveness.* Over time, they appreciate how they can go about modifying and manipulating language to achieve this.

● **Provide access to a wide-range of quality texts**

To enable boys to write skilfully, we also need to ensure that they frequently encounter high-quality texts from a diverse range of voices and genres. As Susan Jones insists:

> it is precisely in their ability to transform and shape ideas through an increased repertoire of linguistic possibilities that writers transform what they know through the act of writing.[35]

To develop this 'repertoire of linguistic possibilities', we need to ensure that we don't just show them great writing, we also unpick the language at sentence, paragraph and whole text level, to interrogate what makes it so.

I love using my own writing in lessons,[36] from magazine articles to rejected and neglected poetry languishing at the bottom of a dusty drawer. Using 'published' texts gives the writing you examine a sense of authenticity that appeals to boys. It also provides opportunities to question the author – i.e. you – on the repertoire of linguistic choices you made. The next step is to 'publish' boys' work – keep it anonymous or pseudonymous so the other students don't know what's going on – and use it as a style model in class. Roy Corden's research backs up this approach:

> We found that children benefit from experiencing what it is like to be an author – wrestling with problems, drawing on knowledge and experiences, seeking advice and responding to critical comments.[37]

I've had success getting boys to create their own 'about the author' bios, to accompany their 'published' work. This is yet another way of raising the profile of creative writing by treating them as authors in their own right.

● Know your male students' personal writing profiles

As I emphasised during Chapter 7, modelling each aspect of the writing process – such as mindmapping story ideas, composing, editing and redrafting – is a vital step towards improving boys' writing techniques. But, at the same time, we have to be aware that there is no one-size-fits-all approach to creative writing. Some famous writers, like J.K. Rowling, draw up plot outlines but will make necessary changes as the narrative unfolds. Others, like the late Terry Pratchett, allow the story to move in its own direction as it goes onto the page. As Susan Jones points out, teachers need to discover where their male students fit on the planning/spontaneity spectrum:

> Understanding personal writing profiles, for example, might reveal that the writer who writes in order to discover what to say may not need to invest time in planning but may well need to spend time revising. Conversely, the writer who revises constantly in order to ensure that the writing generated through translation is in line with the writing intentions of a carefully constructed plan may not need to spend as much time in post-hoc revision.[38]

Encouraging any novice writer to complete at least a basic story outline is a good idea. But there's little to be gained in making boys bash out five pages of detailed planning notes if their time would be better spent editing their free-flowing first draft.

● Allow choice and encourage the development of an individual voice

Much research into boys' motivation and creative writing emphasises the central role that choice plays in keeping them interested in the creative process. Debra Myhill found that:

> More boys, high- and underachievers…appeared to be unmotivated by having to write with a closed purpose, rather than articulating their own ideas and perspectives.[39]

Even where assessment materials seem to be prescriptive, we can still allow boys to have freedom *within* these constraints. Using a rigid tick-off-the-features writing frame, for example, can have a demotivating effect on boys from the outset.

As such, boys can be trained to approach exam writing tasks with a flexible interpretation of what a given story title actually means. For example, 'Write about a time when you got lost' can be tackled metaphorically rather than adhering to the obvious literal meaning. Taught to think like this, boys might write about dubious moral choices they were forced to make, rather than a mundane tale of being inadvertently left behind in the supermarket by their parents.

Check our writing prejudices

As we've seen from research earlier in the chapter, some of these writing restrictions are imposed on boys by teachers – usually female teachers – who recoil at the 'immature' violence and 'detached and humorous style'[40] of much of boys' writing. Linda Peterson argues that 'examining our own gender-linked preferences is a necessary prerequisite to assigning and evaluating students' writing'.[41] That doesn't mean that we shouldn't encourage boys to be more versatile writers by adding stories that focus more on personal reflection and deeper meaning. But, as Peterson sees it, being prejudiced against writing because it features guns and car crashes is a sure-fire way to make boys feel unnoticed and undervalued. Lou Enstone, a secondary English teacher from South East London concurs:

> We have to be careful not to put limits on what our students are allowed to write about. There's a real danger to telling students they can't write about certain things, based on the teacher's comfort zone.[42]

Ban writing topics at your peril. It's a certain way to diminish a boy's enthusiasm for creative writing.

● **Teach boys to write effective action sequences**

CASE STUDY

Lou Enstone, secondary English teacher, South East London

The first thing we need to bear in mind when teaching narrative writing, argues Enstone, is that the pieces we generally ask pupils to write in school aren't really short stories. Short stories are usually quite long! Instead, 'we are asking pupils to write a very specialised type of fiction: what the academics would call flash fiction'.[43] And this type of narrative writing has its own form, structure and language. For this reason, Enstone cautions that 'we have to be careful not to apply novelistic techniques and novelistic expectations to a genre to which they are wholly unsuited.'

As teachers of writing, we often show students examples of great writing from great novels. Yet this risks encouraging students to attempt to shoehorn these novelistic techniques into their 500 word flash fiction with pretty disastrous results. Instead of applying the narrative structure of the novel, Enstone advises, we need to appreciate that the conventions of the very short story should focus on:

■ A definite moment in time

■ Simplicity is key

■ Limited structure

■ Clarity and precision

We've all read 3 page stories where a (usually young male) writer details 24 onomato-poeia-riddled hours of things happening, like characters being chased by a knife-wielding maniac. Or summarises ten years of societal breakdown after the meltdown of a nuclear plant. This interminable thing happens and then this happens and then this happens and so on...

As we've seen, boys like writing action but teachers often reject action writing as lacking literary value. According to Enstone, this is a mistake: 'we have to teach them how to describe deeds, how to describe movement, how to describe gesture. It's a very challenging technical element of writing and we do our students a disservice if we don't teach it.'

So how does Enstone ensure that the boys (and girls) in her class are able to write action effectively?

Improving boys' creative writing tip 1: Develop their vocab through specific focus on verbs and nouns

Don't just assume that boys will automatically use interesting verbs in their writing. By discussing the difference between commonplace, neutral verbs like 'walked' and poten-tially more powerful verbs like 'crouched', 'prowled', 'skulked', 'strode' or 'trampled' we can show boys how to convey far more interesting imagery to their reader.

The same goes for nouns. Show them an image of a man laying bricks on a building site. They might pick out 'hard hat', 'bricks' and 'boots' but, with your assistance in build-ing noun knowledge, they could build up a much more detailed bank of nouns – such as 'lump hammer', 'masonry saw', 'spirit level', 'bolster' and 'scutch tool' – to aid their descriptive passages.

Improving boys' creative writing tip 2: Recreate shot-by-shot scenes

By thinking more precisely about the *exact* type of action, students are able to dramat-ically improve their narratives by breaking down action into minute increments. This means that a moment of action is chunked into five sequential phases, which forces students to think very carefully about what is happening in each micro-section of time. So, for example, instead of 'the car slid on the oil patch and crashed into the wall', we might get a multi-clause slow motion[44] sentence (or sequence) that details things like the buzzing fly on the dashboard and the jerking arms of the windscreen wipers as the car careers towards destruction.

Improving boys' creative writing tip 3: Add urgency or interrupt actions to create tension

As Enstone explains, to move away from clichéd Hollywood narratives, we need to teach 'moments of high drama interrupted by inconsequential actions or dialogue'. This increases tension and adds to the overall atmosphere of urgency. She gives the example of a roller coaster reaching the zenith of the track before preparing to drop down the precipice, only to be interrupted by a small child needing a wee. Urgency can be added through introducing a time-sensitive process, such as a repetitive structural countdown (1 hour to go. 50 minutes to go. 5 minutes to go…). In this way, the sometimes tedious accounts of non-stop action that some boys produce can be made much more effective and interesting to read.

● **Avoid unnecessary 'boy-friendly' writing stimuli**

What's great about Enstone's approach is that it appeals to many boys' narrative interests but the focus generally remains anchored by the written text itself. Where visual stimuli are used, little 'writing time' is wasted, as the focus soon shifts to language and syntax. Unlike Enstone's text-centred method, other uses of writing stimuli tend to fall into the 'boy-friendly' engagement trap, where the stimulus is often used as a way to try and hook reluctant writers in by initially disguising the writing element.

Researchers such as Ellison and Drew, for example, argue that using non-traditional texts in the classroom, 'such as graphic novels, magazines, internet forums, and computer games'[45] can lead to greater engagement and creativity in boys' writing. Their 2020 study asked boys to play *Minecraft*, with the aim being to improve their visualisation, and in turn, descriptive writing skills. As a pre-test, they asked the boys to spend a lesson writing a story after looking at a photograph. The next lesson was spent 60 minutes playing *Minecraft* and chatting about the game in pairs. Finally, a post-test story was written, inspired by their gaming the lesson before. According to the authors:

> the interviews with the students showed students' beliefs that the intervention was positive in developing their creativity…Furthermore, the students signified their sense of excitement and engagement as a result of the intervention.

Minecraft for writing?

The boys told researchers that they thought gaming helped them to write creatively. They enjoyed the gaming lesson and, unsurprisingly, several were keen to play more *Minecraft* but this time would prefer 'the social experience' of interacting in multi-player mode with their peers. When it came to the actual writing, however, the results of the intervention proved to be somewhat modest: 'there was a small improvement in outcomes in the post-test'. The modest impact of this writing intervention might be explained by thinking back to the research on boys and effective revision in Chapter 4. You'll recall that learners, especially boys, tend to instinctively ascribe efficacy to what they are initially more inclined to do, but this doesn't always correlate with higher achievement. The boys in this study conflated creativity and motivation, with little improvement in outcomes.

Furthermore, when thinking of the writing stimuli you might use, it's best to consider the opportunity cost (what else you could have done with the time spent on an activity). Rather than pandering to the stereotypical belief that boys prefer gaming to writing, might a 5-minute tour on Google Street View, or indeed an evocative description of Castle Dracula have done the trick instead?

To get boys to write well, we need to give them the tools to succeed. Deconstruct what makes good writing. Give them the technical tools, and freedom of choice, to try these features in their own writing. Have high expectations of what they can achieve, by focusing on the writing as the main thing. And then allow them lots of opportunities to put their new ideas and techniques into practice.

How can I improve boys' creative writing?

STEPS TO SUCCESS

1 EMBRACE Embrace terminology and grammar

2 INSPIRE Inspire through wordplay and fun activities

3 PLANNING Know boys' planning and drafting preferences

4 CHOICE Allow them choice over genre

5 ACTION Show them how to write action effectively

Notes

1 Standard attainment tests - statutory assessments carried out at different stage of a child's primary school education in England.
2 The official term for a child who achieves a scaled score of 110 or above.
3 Department for Education. (2019) 'National curriculum assessments at key stage 2 in England'. Available at: https://assets.publishing.service.gov.uk/government/uploads/system/uploads/attachment_data/file/830285/KS2_Provisional_publication_text_2019.pdf (Accessed 1 July 2020).
4 Allen-Kinross, P. (2019) 'GCSE results 2019: Girls still lead the way over boys', *Schools Week*, 22 August 2019. Available at: https://schoolsweek.co.uk/gcse-results-2019-girls-still-lead-the-way-over-boys/#:~:text=Girls%20are%20continuing%20to%20outperform,3.9%20per%20cent%20for%20boys (Accessed 3 July 2020).
5 Myhill, D. (2001) 'Writing: crafting and creating', *English in Education*, 35:3, pp. 13–20.
6 For further reading on this aspect of how poor verbal literacy impacts on emotional literacy, relationships and mental health, see Chapter 4 and Chapter 9 of Pinkett, M., & Roberts, M. (2019) *Boys Don't Try? Rethinking Masculinity in Schools*, Abingdon, Oxon: Routledge.
7 I find the distinction between these two 'types' of writing an odd one. Most decent short pieces of fiction have some description and some narrative, so there's an inevitable crossover between the two.
8 Ibid.
9 Peterson, L.H. (1991) 'Gender and the autobiographical essay: research perspectives, pedagogical practices', *College Composition and Communication*, 42:2, pp. 170–183.

10 Faigley, L. (1989) 'Judging writing, judging selves', *College Composition and Communication*, 40, pp. 395–412.

11 Graves, D.H. (1973) 'Sex differences in children's writing', *Elementary English*, 50:7, pp. 1101–1106.

12 Ibid.

13 Franklin, J. (2001) 'Helping Ophelia *and* Hamlet: how teachers can develop boys' interests in literature', *ASCD Curriculum Update*: Summer 2001, pp. 4–5.

14 Ibid.

15 Anderson, M. (2003) 'Reading violence in boys' writing', *Language Arts*, 80:3, pp. 223–231.

16 Peterson, S. (1998) 'Evaluation and teachers' perceptions of gender in sixth-grade student writing', *Research in the Teaching of English*, 33:2, pp. 181–208.

17 Newkirk, T. (2000) 'Misreading masculinity: speculations on the great gender gap in writing', *Language Arts*, 77: 4, pp. 294–300.

18 Ibid.

19 Millard, E. (1997) *Differently Literate: Boys, Girls and the Schooling of Literacy*, London: Falmer Press.

20 Ibid.

21 Ibid.

22 Fitzpatrick, L. (2019) 'Male teachers ruling out primary school jobs because they fear being viewed with suspicion', The Telegraph, 13 January 2019. Available at: https://www.telegraph.co.uk/news/2019/01/13/male-primary-teachers-speak-fears-perceived-suspicious-working/ (Accessed 8 July 2020).

23 Ibid.

24 Graham, S., Bollinger, A., Olson, C.B., D'Aoust, C., MacArthur, C., McCutchen, D., & Olinghouse, N. (2012) *Teaching Elementary School Students to be Effective Writers*, United States of America: Institute of Education Sciences, pp. 1–103.

25 Puranik, C., Al Otaiba, S., Folsom, J., & Greulich, L. (2014) 'Exploring the amount and type of writing instruction during language arts instruction in kindergarten classrooms', *Reading and Writing,* 27: 2, pp. 213–236.

26 Jones, S. (2014) 'From ideas in the head to words on the page: young adolescents' reflections on their own writing processes', *Language and Education*, 28:1, pp. 52–67.

27 Ibid.

28 Andrews, R. (2005) 'Knowledge about the teaching of [sentence] grammar: The state of play', *English Teaching: Practice and Critique*, 4:3, pp. 69–76.

29 Corden, R. (2007) 'Developing reading-writing connections: the impact of explicit instruction of literary devices on the quality of children's narrative writing', *Journal of Research in Childhood Education*, 21:3, pp. 269–289.

30 Myhill, D.A., Jones, S.M., Lines, H., & Watson, A. (2012) 'Re-thinking grammar: the impact of embedded grammar teaching on students' writing and students' metalinguistic understanding', *Research Papers in Education*, 27:2, pp. 139–166.

31 Try it again but say it quickly.

32 This amusing device, where a speaker mixes up the opening sound of a pair of words, is called a spoonerism.

33 For a more detailed discussion of cliché and writing, see Roberts, M. (2016) 'We need to talk about clichés (part 1)'. Available at: https://markrobertsteach.wordpress.com/2016/08/28/we-need-to-talk-about-cliches-part-1/ (Accessed 10th July 2020).

34 Leonard, E. (2007) *Elmore Leonard's 10 Rules of Writing*, New York: William Morrow & Company.

35 Ibid.

36 For more on this, see Roberts, M. (2017) 'Here's one I made earlier: Using your own creative writing as literary texts'. Available at: https://markrobertsteach.wordpress.com/2017/03/28/heres-one-i-made-earlier-using-your-own-creative-writing-as-literary-texts/ (Accessed 3 July 2020).

37 Ibid.

38 Ibid.

39 Ibid.

40 Hallden, G. (1999) ''To be, or not to be': absurd and humoristic descriptions as a strategy to avoid idyllic life stories- boys write about family life', *Gender and Education*, 11:4, pp. 469–479.

41 Ibid.

42 Enstone, L. (2020) 'Action writing! Helping pupils write effective action sequences in fiction – bring on the blood, the gore, and the disaster stories!', Team English National Conference, Saturday 4 July 2020, delivered online.

43 Ibid.

44 Writing experts often call slow motion writing 'extended time'.

45 Ellison, M., & Drew, C. (2020) 'Using digital sandbox gaming to improve creativity within boys' writing', *Journal of Research in Childhood Education*, 34:2, pp. 277–287.

The final word

The ultimate aim of a charity, my wife often reminds me, is to make itself redundant. Having worked her entire career in the charitable sector, she's all too aware of the paradox that were an organisation to achieve its primary objective, it would become unnecessary. Its work fulfilled, the charity would no longer be required.

In writing this book, I hope to make myself redundant. Nothing would give greater satisfaction than seeing my advice about how to deal with the boy question implemented in schools and classrooms across the land. Taught effectively, and taught how best to learn, I feel certain that boys will succeed academically. Gaps will narrow; boys' attitudes to learning will change for the better; concern about the societal impact of male academic underachievement will diminish.

Then I can stop writing books about boys and start focusing on other important educational topics. No longer will I need to be "the boy guy".

It sounds utopian, doesn't it? Like a rare disease cured or homeless charity that has nobody left to house. Yet, it's my sincere belief that closing gender attainment gaps is a realistic, achievable objective. In reading this book, I know you share that belief. I know you believe that teaching can make a difference to the life chances of the boys you teach. And, most of all, I know that you will continue to strive until the boy question goes away.

So take the ideas from this book and help boys soar. It's time to put me out of a job.

Index

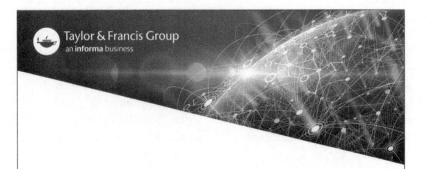